Raising an Anxious Child

This book offers a lifeline to parents raising children with anxiety, combining expert insights with real-life experiences to create a resource that is both informative and relatable.

Follow the inspiring journey of Rose and her mother Rachel as they navigate the complex and often overwhelming world of special education. Drawing on first-hand accounts, this book enables parents to understand what anxiety is and how to navigate the challenges of the special education system. Each chapter not only shares the real-life struggles and victories of Rose's journey but also provides practical advice and actionable strategies for parents facing similar challenges. Whether it's understanding special education terminology, advocating for accommodations, or finding the right educational environment, this book will empower you with the tools and confidence needed to nurture your anxious child with compassion and empathy.

Whether you're new to this process or looking to deepen your understanding, this resource provides parents and educators with everything they need to work together to create meaningful change and ensure that every child has the opportunity to thrive.

Rachel Krueger has been an advocate for those affected by mental health challenges and learning disabilities for over 20 years. She has worked to raise awareness and emphasizes the importance of educating others to support those in need.

Beverley H. Johns has been a special educator for many years and was a Professional Fellow at MacMurray College. She is the author of over 30 books and currently serves as the President of the Learning Disabilities Association of Illinois.

Raising an Anxious Child

A Parent and Educator's Perspective

Rachel Krueger and Beverley H. Johns

Taylor & Francis Group
NEW YORK AND LONDON

Designed cover image: Getty images

First published 2026
by Routledge
605 Third Avenue, New York, NY 10158

and by Routledge
4 Park Square, Milton Park, Abingdon, Oxon, OX14 4RN

Routledge is an imprint of the Taylor & Francis Group, an informa business

© 2026 Rachel Krueger and Beverley H. Johns

The right of Rachel Krueger and Beverley H. Johns to be identified as authors of this work has been asserted in accordance with sections 77 and 78 of the Copyright, Designs and Patents Act 1988.

All rights reserved. No part of this book may be reprinted or reproduced or utilised in any form or by any electronic, mechanical, or other means, now known or hereafter invented, including photocopying and recording, or in any information storage or retrieval system, without permission in writing from the publishers.

For Product Safety Concerns and Information please contact our EU representative GPSR@taylorandfrancis.com. Taylor & Francis Verlag GmbH, Kaufingerstraße 24, 80331 München, Germany.

Trademark notice: Product or corporate names may be trademarks or registered trademarks, and are used only for identification and explanation without intent to infringe.

ISBN: 978-1-041-04655-4 (pbk)
ISBN: 978-1-003-62931-3 (ebk)

DOI: 10.4324/9781003629313

Illustrations by Nick Manker at Production Xpress

Typeset in Adobe Caslon Pro
by SPi Technologies India Pvt Ltd (Straive)

Access the Support Material: www.routledge.com/ 9781041046554

Contents

Acknowledgements vi
Introduction vii
About This Book viii

CHAPTER 1 The Journey Begins 1
CHAPTER 2 Big Girl School 5
CHAPTER 3 The Challenge of Second Grade with an Anxiety
             Diagnosis 11
CHAPTER 4 What's a 504 Plan? 22
CHAPTER 5 From 504 to an IEP 29
CHAPTER 6 Middle School Challenges 33
CHAPTER 7 The Charter School Experience 40
CHAPTER 8 Pursuing Outlets for Anxiety 48
CHAPTER 9 The Complexity of Anxiety 54
CHAPTER 10 Making Connections 59
CHAPTER 11 Planning Ahead for Difficult Situations 65
CHAPTER 12 Coping with Communication Breakdowns 69
CHAPTER 13 The Importance of Endurance for Success 80

Appendix 85
Bibliography 98

Acknowledgements

Thank you to the Learning Disabilities Association of America for bringing us together to write this book.

Thank you to all the parents and educators who work together to advocate for the needs of students with anxiety, thank you for supporting our kids.

Thank you to all students who struggle with anxiety, may we always be there for them.

Thank you to our family for their encouragement and support in helping us write this book.

Lastly, on a personal note, I (Rachel) want to thank my daughter, Rose, for allowing me to share your story. You Love I.

Introduction

Many years ago, when Bev first began her special education teaching career, she had a student named Sally who came to her classroom for the first time at the age of ten years. Her mother, who lived in southern Illinois and had ten children, took Sally to school to register her. The school principal looked at Sally and said, "She cannot come to school. She has too many problems." Her mother brought her back home. You see, Sally had significant intellectual disabilities: she had autism, she had cerebral palsy, she had an unrepaired cleft palate, she had significant behavioral problems, and she did not talk.

When Sally was ten, a law had passed in Illinois (the precursor to the first federal mandate for special education, Public Law 94-142) that said that all students with disabilities had the right to go to school, regardless of the severity of their disability. Thus, Sally entered Bev's classroom, and they began the journey to reach her. Sally was taken to a well-renowned hospital for an evaluation and got her cleft palate repaired. She thrived in school, did not have behavioral problems, and began talking. Every day, Bev thinks of Sally and how much more progress we could have made with her if we had only gotten to start services when she was three years of age. Sally drives the special education advocacy work that Bev does because she never wants to see a child be denied services like Sally was.

Yet today, countless parents report that their children are not getting the services they should receive. While we have accomplished a lot, we have miles to go before we sleep.

About This Book

Raising an Anxious Child tells a profound story that elicits a call to action to empower parents to advocate on behalf of their children. This book chronicles how another child in today's world struggled to get the services she needed despite her mother's tireless efforts and persistent advocacy at the school. The maze of services, the barriers to understanding special education, and the reluctance of school district personnel to provide students with necessary services still persist.

Rachel felt compelled to share what her family endured with other parents who have faced or are facing similar issues. She speaks from a parent perspective and has enlisted the help of her friend and co-author, Bev, to provide takeaways for educators they can implement in the classroom. It also shows how families and educators can collaborate for the betterment of a child. Meaningful change is possible when parents, educators, and the school work together.

As you turn the page, you will find stories that will move you, insights that will empower you, and tools that will help you navigate the complex world of special education. Together, we can ensure that no child is ever denied the services they need to succeed.

Let's begin this journey together.

Chapter 1

The Journey Begins

Rachel's Story

Rose was a rambunctious little girl who loved to explore the world around her. With two older siblings whom she adored, she was always trying to keep up with them. She had a fierce energy about her and an attitude to match. She was a force to be reckoned with! Rose was not your typical third child, as she was so strong-willed and she knew what she wanted. She sometimes ignored what we told her to do when given simple tasks. It always seemed such a chore for her, but we later discovered there was a reason for her behavior. Rose's determination, although sometimes frustrating, was also a testament to her independence.

As Rose grew older, we noticed she had trouble expressing herself clearly. At times, her speech was difficult to understand. It was a relief that her older sister seemed to have a special knack for understanding what she was trying to communicate. Although I know that comparing children is not recommended, Rose's speech issues were on another level.

One day when I was volunteering at my older children's school, I mentioned Rose's speech delays to my older daughter's teacher. She suggested making an appointment at the school with the speech pathologist to have her tested, and that there would be no cost. She told me that all public schools had many different options for testing children and that it was free for any family. I discussed with my husband what I had learned and he thought it was something we should do. I had not considered testing Rose, who was almost three at the time, but I thought it couldn't hurt and we could get some answers to our questions.

The next day, I called the elementary school my two older children were attending to see if they offered any kind of testing. I was told, in fact, that they did, and we needed to make an appointment with the Speech Pathologist, and the evaluation would take place at the school.

The following week, I received an email form the speech pathologist, and she let me know she had an opening the next day. I made the appointment and she told me what I needed to do to prepare for Rose to be tested. I was so thankful to my daughter's teacher for telling us this was an option as we would not have even thought to have Rose tested.

We got to the school at Rose's scheduled testing time, and she walked down the hall to a classroom for her hearing and speech tests. We were told it would take about thirty minutes and we could wait in the lobby. I knew it was better if we were not in the room with her, but just looking at how little she was in that classroom, made me want to go in there and give her a big hug!

One week later, we got the test results back and were relieved to find out that Rose did not have any speech or hearing issues, but we were still puzzled about why we were having a hard time understanding her. My husband and I still felt that something was off, but as far as testing went, we were told that was all they could do for her. We accepted the results and decided we would seek further guidance if we needed to have her tested again in the future.

What's a Parent to Do?

When Rachel started to notice that Rose was having difficulty in the speech and language area, she did not deny it or try to say she would outgrow it. Sometimes parents think their child will outgrow a problem and they may, but most parents want to help their child at the earliest age possible. Early intervention is the key to success and

Rose was showing signs of delays that worried Rachel. As a result she asked her older daughter's teacher, who told her accurately that the school could evaluate Rose at no cost to the parent. That was correct. Under the child find provisions of the Individuals with Disabilities Education Act, school districts are responsible for seeking out children who may be delayed in development or are having other issues that are of concern. The testing done ruled out that there was a medical problem—her hearing was intact. A parent always wants to rule out whether there is a visual or auditory acuity problem. The evaluation also showed that Rose did not have a speech disorder. Speech can impact early reading so this is something that Rachel was concerned about.

As parents, you are your child's strongest advocate. Trust your instincts, ask questions, and seek support if something doesn't feel right. Early intervention can make a significant difference, and there are many resources available to help your child thrive, whether through schools, medical professionals, or community programs.

If you're concerned about the costs of testing, please know that support is available regardless of your financial situation. Don't hesitate to reach out to your pediatrician, school district, or local organizations for guidance. Remember, early intervention is crucial, and there are people and programs ready to support you every step of the way.

Table 1.1
Your early intervention roadmap

Action	Why it's important
Observation	Pay attention to how your child communicates, interacts, and responds to instructions. Delays in speech, difficulty following directions, or frustration when trying to express themselves may be signs of concern.
Understanding IDEA	The Individuals with Disabilities Education Act (IDEA) ensures that children with developmental delays have access to services. Parents should familiarize themselves with their rights under this law. Every state has a federally funded Parent Training and Information Center that helps parents understand IDEA and advocate for their children. Visit www.parentcenterhub.org/find-your-center to find a PTI in your state.

(Continued)

Table 1.1
(Continued)

Action	Why it's important
Consultation	Teachers, caregivers, or pediatricians can provide valuable insights and may suggest next steps.
Evaluation	Early testing can rule out medical issues and identify areas needing support. Evaluations are often free through public schools and can provide critical information about your child's development. Testing may include speech, hearing, and cognitive assessments.
Next steps	If testing doesn't provide answers, but concerns persist, consider seeking further evaluation through private specialists or developmental clinics.

Takeaways

1. Every school district is responsible for the child-find obligation of the Individuals with Disabilities Education Act of 2004. Schools are required to look for children who may need assistance. Schools put notices in the news or on the web and provide teams of individuals who are able to evaluate children at no cost to the parents. They go into day care centers, set up screening clinics, to make screenings and further evaluations accessible to all families.

2. Early intervention is key for children. If a parent suspects their child is having difficulty with developmental milestones, they should get it checked. It is sometimes too easy to think that the child will outgrow a problem. While they may, they may also not outgrow it, and the earlier we identify a problem the better.

3. It is important to rule out a medical problem with the child, ensuring they do not have hearing or vision loss. It is also important to rule out any underlying medical issues as they can sometimes mimic or exacerbate developmental delays. Addressing these possibilities early helps create a clearer picture of the child's needs. By combining medical and educational evaluations, families and schools can work together to support children effectively.

Chapter 2
Big Girl School

Rachel's Story

Rose's journey into public school began in 2007, and she was excited to be in a "big girl school" just like her older siblings. We decided to let her start school at age five, even though she had a summer birthday. That meant that she would be in class with kids who were possibly almost one year older than her. My husband and I discussed whether she should start this year or wait until the following year to enroll her. However, we felt like she was ready as she did well in pre-school, and her teachers felt she was ready. I was happy that all three of my kids would attend the same school for the next year. Of course, it helped my heart to know that Rose would see her siblings every day.

Rose had a kind and nurturing kindergarten teacher who provided her with love and guidance. She loved going to school every day, and she seemed to be thriving. However, her teacher informed us that Rose struggled with reading during the early part of the year. Her teacher sent her home with practice books that would help Rose become a stronger reader. A lot had changed since my other two kids were in kindergarten, as reading was not part of their curriculum. This meant that Rose was already behind and would need more support. We continued to work with her at home, practicing her letters and reading books. My husband and I were hopeful Rose would be able to get back on track and continue making progress with her reading proficiency.

In the spring, Rose's teacher announced that she was pregnant and might be unable to finish the year. While I was thrilled for her, I also knew that Rose had made a strong connection with her, as she understood the best way to teach her. When she told the parents who her long-term substitute teacher would be, I was very happy, as she was someone I respected and had been a substitute for my other kids. She had become a friend, and she knew Rose very well.

Rose's interim teacher saw that she was still struggling with reading and mentioned that we should build up her confidence by providing books at a lower level. We tried that for a couple of weeks to see if that would help. However, it became apparent that Rose needed more assistance than we could offer her, and we knew the teacher could not spend all her time attending to Rose's needs. After talking with her teacher, we decided to look for a tutor and found Kumon, a program that helps kids with reading and math.

We signed Rose up for four weeks of tutoring to get her the help she needed in reading. After starting the program, Rose began to enjoy reading more, and we noticed that she was making significant progress. She wanted to read all the time, and she was actually enjoying her reading homework. Kumon seemed to give her the boost she needed to feel more confident.

Her teacher sent us an email asking us to come to the school for a meeting. We had not heard from her in a couple of weeks, so we thought Rose's reading problem was resolved, but we were wrong. She was still having a hard time, and was making progress, but was not at the level she needed to be in order for her to move on to the first grade. Rose was doing well in the rest of her studies, and her teacher recommended continuing Kumon tutoring over the summer to prepare her for the upcoming year.

Rose continued her twice-weekly tutoring sessions over the summer, and she seemed to develop a newfound confidence. Gone was the little girl who was shy about reading out loud. She asked us to take her to the bookstore so she could pick out new books. We could only hope this would translate to the upcoming school year, and she would breeze through first grade.

Summer flew by and it was time for Rose to begin first grade. We felt very optimistic about the progress she made in reading and going to tutoring at Kumon, but that optimism was short-lived. It was not long before we were called in to see her teacher. She told us that Rose was struggling in math and reading. What? She was doing so well in both subjects, so what happened? In her writing, her sentences were not complex enough. Did I miss something? How was a six-year-old supposed to write complex sentences? Once again, we relied on Kumon, and this time, we added math. Rose was a little more reluctant to return there because she felt she already knew how to read and she was confused about why math was being added. This became our struggle three days a week, as this made Rose very sad.

Not long after school started, as had happened the previous school year, Rose's teacher shared the wonderful news that she was expecting a baby. I was genuinely thrilled for her and tried to focus on the positive, even though I knew it would mean some changes ahead. Thankfully, her long-term substitute was fantastic and she was a friend of mine, which gave me a lot of comfort. I knew she cared about Rose and would keep me informed about anything my girl needed.

While I was happy to have a friendly face as the substitute teacher, she had an emergency arise, and she too needed to step away. This would be Rose's third teacher for first grade. Although this was not the ideal situation, I tried to remain optimistic for her sake. This was another challenge, but I hoped this transition would still offer Rose the care and consistency she needed to thrive.

I decided it was best to go to the school to meet the second substitute teacher who would be taking over and to provide her with some background information about Rose and how she learns best. She seemed like a caring person, but I was unsure of her qualifications and if she would be able to provide Rose with the support she needed.

She was not one of the substitutes any of my children had before, so this would be a learning curve for us. I asked her to email or call me with any questions or concerns. I wanted to make sure Rose was getting the attention and guidance she deserved.

Spring had arrived, and I was beyond relieved when I received an email saying that Rose's original teacher would be returning from maternity leave with a little more than two months left in the school year. We were all ready to be done with the ups and downs of first grade, and I felt a huge sense of relief knowing Rose would be back with a familiar face. I could not help but think ahead to next year and was determined to make sure Rose had a teacher who was focused and ready for the year ahead, preferably someone who was not planning any significant life changes!

During Rose's first two years of school, her kindergarten and first-grade teachers announced their pregnancies. While I was truly happy for them, I knew their time away from the classroom presented some challenges for Rose. I wanted to ensure continuity in her education, so I reached out to the principal with a request to have Rose placed with a teacher I was familiar with for second grade. She had also taught my son, although there had been some challenges, I knew she was capable and experienced. In hindsight, it was not the right fit for Rose, but given the timing, it was important to make a decision quickly. The principal had the final say, and I hoped for the best in Rose's second grade year.

What's A Parent To Do?

Because we live in a day and age of teacher shortages, Rachel's experience is not unusual today. Teachers are absent or are out on maternity leave and some children have difficulty adjusting to new teachers. Positive relationships with teachers are critical to a child's success and you saw this as Rachel explained Rose's relationships with her teachers.

You also saw where Rose's speech difficulties were impacting her reading. Rachel also studied who the teachers were in the buildings and requested a specific teacher for Rose as she went into second grade. Parents cannot choose the teacher that is assigned to his or her child but the parent can certainly provide input as Rachel did. She was being proactive.

Throughout Rose's first two years, Rachel maintained consistent communication with the teachers, ensuring she was fully aware of what was happening with Rose. Rachel was being proactive which meant she was always informed about her child's progress and any challenges she was facing in school. It was important for Rachel to stay involved as keeping the lines of communication open helped establish a strong partnership with the school and Rose's teachers. It was important that Rachel stayed involved in Rose's time at school and was able to share important information with the teachers. It was also vital that she kept the lines of communication open to help establish a strong partnership between Rachel and the educators. It also fostered a collaborative environment where Rose's needs were prioritized and addressed effectively.

Table 2.1
Your roadmap for teacher collaboration

Action	Why it's important
Build positive relationships with teachers	Strong teacher–student relationships are critical for academic and emotional success. Encourage your child to connect with their teacher.
Provide input on teacher assignments	While you can't choose your child's teacher, you can share insights about your child's needs and preferences.
Maintain consistent communication and involvement	Staying informed will ensure you are aware of your child's progress and challenges. Schedule regular check-ins with teachers, use email or school portals to stay updated, and attend parent-teacher conferences.
Advocate for your child's needs	Positive advocacy helps ensure your child receives the support they need to thrive. Monitor your child's progress and speak up about concerns or needed accommodations.

Takeaways

1. Keep the door open to communication with your child's teacher. Remember that you know more about your child than they do and you have valuable insight to share.
2. Recognize that there may be substitutes in classes for a variety of reasons and it will be important for you to share information with each of them. You cannot assume one teacher will always communicate with another.
3. When your child is struggling you may want to consider tutoring options or further evaluation.

Chapter 3

The Challenge of Second Grade with an Anxiety Diagnosis

Rachel's Story

Rose was looking forward to second grade, and we were happy with the principal's decision to accept my request to have a hand in choosing her teacher. I was also at ease, as I had firsthand experience with this teacher's approach as to how she taught her students, and I thought Rose would benefit from her experience. She was a firm but supportive teacher, and I had high hopes that Rose would thrive in her classroom. I felt confident that, despite the challenges of Rose's previous years, she could provide the stability and structure she needed to succeed in second grade.

Her teacher gave each child a task folder at the beginning of the year. If the student stayed on green and had no write-ups in their folder, they would get a prize at the end of the week. Rose was not a child who caused trouble for teachers or anyone else. But, in this class with this particular teacher, she would be written up almost daily.

Her dad and I were perplexed. Some of the infractions were her talking while the teacher was speaking, not paying attention, taking her jacket on and off too many times, and going to the bathroom too much. You read that correctly. I understand if a child asks to go to the bathroom too many times in an hour, but I do not understand the situation with the jacket. I requested to have a conference with said teacher to discuss these issues.

In our meeting, she mentioned that Rose was continuously putting on and removing her jacket and that became a distraction in class. She also noted that Rose went to the bathroom a lot. I thought that was strange, as I do not recall Rose having to go to the bathroom often when we were at home.

My husband and I were concerned, and we discussed what to do next. It was decided to take her to her pediatrician to have her tested to determine if there was anything wrong. Little did I know this would open a whole new world for us.

I made the appointment to see her doctor and was told it would be a couple of weeks. My main concern was that she could possibly have diabetes. Her dad and I did not notice any of the typical symptoms of the disease, but we felt it was important to get answers to make sure she was not sick or that we had not missed any signs of her being unwell. Diabetes did not run in either of our families, but we felt it best to have Rose tested just to be sure. The uncertainty was nerve-wracking, as this was completely unexpected, but we knew getting her tested would give us the peace of mind we needed.

The day arrived for her appointment, a day I had been dreading. What if my baby had diabetes or worse? How could this diagnosis have been missed in the first seven years of her life? My mind raced with worry as we made our way to the doctor's office. We checked in at the reception desk, and I was given new forms to fill out. The questions about her health and what had changed felt like an interrogation, each one making me question whether I had missed something important. As far as her father and I knew, nothing had changed, as she seemed healthy and full of energy, just as she always had been. Still, I filled out the forms with a sense of dread, hoping the answers would bring clarity. My heart was pounding as I sat down to Rose while we waited for her name to be called.

Within a few minutes, the nurse called Rose's name. He asked her to give a urine sample and for me to take her to the bathroom before we entered the room. I grabbed the cup and took her into the restroom. Rose started to panic about having to use the cup for her sample. She tried to go to the bathroom, but nothing happened. She continued to try and would get visibly upset every time. She was crying so hard that I had to stop because she was inconsolable. I asked her what was wrong and she told me she could not do it. She had a mental block. She kept saying, "What will they think of me that I cannot go to the bathroom in the cup? Will they be mad at me?" She wiped her eyes and continued to ask the same question repeatedly. I told her it was alright and no one was mad at her for not being able to give a sample. I asked her if I could take her home and she could try there. She felt better with that suggestion, so I asked the nurse if I could run her home to get the sample and return it. The nurse looked a little puzzled but he obliged me.

We quickly ran home, took her into the bathroom, and got the sample. She was calm and cooperative, and it was a relief to see her ready to return to the doctor's office. Once we arrived, they took us back into the room, and I handed them her sample. The nurse came back, took her vitals, and asked a few more questions. The waiting felt endless, but within a few minutes, we had the test results—negative. Her diabetes test was negative! A huge wave of relief washed over me as I processed the news, and I could not wait to tell my husband!

After speaking with her doctor, she suggested we consider seeing a developmental pediatrician to test for ADHD (attention deficit hyperactivity disorder). ADHD? It was a suggestion we had not even considered for Rose, but as we thought it over, we realized it made sense to explore all possibilities. We knew we owed it to Rose to get a clearer understanding of what might be affecting her while in class. Though it was another step into the unknown, we were ready to take it for her sake, hoping that finding answers would help Rose receive the support she needed.

I began the arduous search looking for a developmental pediatrician. I did not know where to start and I had mixed feelings about why we needed to find one in the first place. All I knew was what her doctor shared with me, and that we needed answers for Rose. I called a few offices, and to my surprise, the waiting lists were incredibly long—ranging from several months to a full year. Frustration began to set in, but I kept pushing forward, determined to get Rose the help she needed.

After discussing the different options with my husband, we finally decided on a developmental pediatrician that seemed like a good fit, though there was an eight-month wait. I called the office, explained the situation, and asked to be placed on the waiting list. The receptionist assured me that we could bring Rose in at any time if there was an earlier opening. I told her that if Rose needed to miss school for the appointment, that would be perfectly fine and getting her in sooner was our top priority. I was relieved knowing we had secured a spot on the list, though my relief turned to worry as I didn't know how long we'd have to wait for answers. Still, we were determined to do whatever it took to get the right help for Rose.

We received a call that there was an opening available after only a couple of months. I quickly reserved the time, and I felt a huge sigh of relief and gratitude that we were finally going to see someone who could help give us answers. It felt like such a long wait, and now it was finally happening.

As it was explained to me, Rose would be testing for at least six hours. I was baffled as to how they were going to be able to hold her attention for that long, but I was reassured she would be in good hands. I did not know what to expect at the appointment, so I packed Rose some snacks and a drink, as I was told she would have some breaks during the day.

I made sure to fully explain to Rose what her appointment would entail. I told her that this was an important step and that we were doing it to better understand how we could help her feel more comfortable while she was at school. As we walked into the office, I could sense Rose was nervous, as was I. Six hours of testing was a long time, and I was not sure how she would be able to handle being in an office for so long. I knew the process would be challenging, but knowing we were taking an important step forward helped ease my fears. I knew this would give us the clarity we needed and was hopeful that it would bring us some answers we were so desperately seeking.

The waiting room door opened, and the nurse called Rose's name. We were taken to a room with a desk, two chairs, and a computer. This would be the room that my little girl would be in for hours. I kissed her goodbye and was told I needed to go to another room down the hall. I was reassured that she would be okay and that they would give her breaks to see me and get a snack. I smiled at Rose and told her I loved her and that I would see her soon.

I was escorted to a room down the hall from Rose. It had a large couch and a television. The nurse told me I needed to watch a video in order to have Rose tested. I thought that was odd, but of course, I agreed. Anything to take my mind off of her going through the hours of testing was welcomed. The video began, and I started to giggle as the music and video seemed like they were from the 1980s! She told me the recording was old, but the message was still the same. I asked her what the name of the video was, and she told me "F.A.T. City." Fat City? I wondered if I had misheard her. She said yes, it is "F. A.T. City," and it stood for "Frustration, Anxiety, and Tension." The actual title was, "How Difficult Can This Be? The F. A. T. City Workshop by Rick Lavoie." I still did not understand why I needed to watch this video or how it pertained to Rose, but I obliged. I settled onto the comfy couch and watched the hour-long video.

After finishing the video, I was amazed at how the speaker really brought you in and put you in the position of a student who needs extra help in school. It highlighted children with learning disabilities and their daily struggles with frustration, anxiety, and tension. The video was eye opening, and it was great to see how each situation was handled and to see the reactions of the teachers as they played the part of the student. To see them play out in a real classroom setting helps create empathy and helps build a more compassionate, informed approach to teaching.

I waited patiently for Rose to come out for her first break in testing. After what seemed like hours, the door finally opened, and she came running down the hall towards me with a big smile on her face. I had packed her some snacks and something to drink and I knew she was ready for some food. I asked what she had been doing in the room and she told me that they were playing games and having fun. It warmed my heart to hear her say that, especially since she would have to go back to that room and play more games. It was a relief to know she was enjoying herself despite the long testing session.

It was time for her to go back to finish her testing. She disappeared down the hall again for a couple more hours, and as I waited, I could not help but feel a sense of pride. Rose seemed to be handling everything so well. As I sat there in my room, I could not help but feel hopeful that we would soon have more clarity about how to best support her.

Once Rose had finished her testing, we made our way back to the room where I had been sitting all day. The doctor instructed us to wait there while they compiled and analyzed the data they had collected from her testing. I was eager to learn what the results were and what we could do to help our little girl.

The doctor called us into her office, and as soon as we walked in, Rose noticed a dog lying in the corner. She was elated as she loved dogs. While the pup kept Rose entertained, I focused on the doctor and what she had to say. What followed was a revelation. Rose had been diagnosed with several conditions—Anxiety, CAPD (central auditory processing disorder), and ADHD. I only knew what ADHD was and had heard of anxiety, but I could not imagine her having this at seven years old. The doctor explained each diagnosis in detail and how they impacted Rose's daily life. It all began to make sense, and we finally had answers to our questions. I was thankful, relieved, and unsure of what to do next. I read over the doctor's reports from her testing, and I was still baffled by the diagnoses Rose had been given.

What was I to do with this information? Who was supposed to help her in school?

Now that we had some answers, it was time for me to share the news with Rose's teacher. I was not prepared for what happened next. When I told her about Rose's diagnoses, she seemed surprised. She told me that she did not quite understand how anxiety was affecting Rose, but I could see that she was open to learning more. I reminded her that she told me about Rose spending more time in the restroom. Now, with the diagnosis, it made sense—anxiety. Her teacher still was not sure that was the reason, but, rest assured, it was.

I spoke with Rose about her time in the bathroom, and she shared that she went there to cry. My heart broke as she told me and I could not imagine how overwhelmed she must have felt day in and day out. Rose must have been struggling with her emotions for a while, and I only wished I would have seen the red flags. She was only seven for goodness sake and that is a lot for a little girl to deal with. Although I was sad for her, we were grateful for the diagnosis that provided us with clarity.

I recognized that Rose's teacher had a very direct teaching style, and I understood why I had chosen her—she had been a great fit for my son, and I had hoped she would offer stability for Rose. While her teacher was committed and dedicated, it became clear that Rose's needs required a different approach. I spoke to her teacher and asked if she thought Rose would benefit from more support. I was ready to work together with her to find strategies that would help her feel more comfortable and confident in the classroom.

My husband and I navigated through Rose's anxiety diagnosis and her other learning issues while working with her teacher throughout the year. While we faced challenges, we did appreciate that she was the one who first noticed Rose was struggling in the classroom. Her observations were what prompted us to visit Rose's pediatrician, which set us on this new path of trying to understand her needs.

We came up with a plan to work with her teacher to identify areas where Rose was facing difficulties. At times, it was not always smooth as this was new to all of us. Sometimes it felt like progress was slow, and we were uncertain about what would work for her. We appreciated the teacher's insights as they are what helped her get the support she needed.

Second grade was quickly coming to an end, and I knew I needed to write another letter to the principal requesting a teacher for third grade. I wanted someone who would be able to understand how Rose learns best and teach to her strengths. I shared with her Rose's experiences with her previous teachers and the areas where she struggled. I had hoped the principal would take that into account since she had a rocky second grade year. I also expressed my hope that the principal would consider my request and place Rose with a teacher who could provide the support she needed; preferably someone who had taught children that learn differently.

I was thrilled to learn that the principal granted my request and gave me my first choice for a teacher. My husband and I felt a sense of relief and optimism, knowing that we were taking a step in the right direction. We felt confident that Rose would have a great year with this teacher as she was someone who was recommended to us. I did not know her personally, but I was told she would have the right approach to supporting students with learning challenges. We felt hopeful that, with the right guidance and understanding, Rose could make positive progress in third grade and begin to truly thrive.

What's A Parent To Do?

There is so much information in this chapter that points to the important role the parent plays and how parents must monitor their child's progress or lack of it in the classroom. Rachel thought she was making a good decision when she asked for the second-grade teacher only to realize this was not the teacher for Rose.

This happens to all of us at one time. We think we are making a good decision in the best interests of the child and it turns out it was not. We cannot foresee the future. We can only do what we believe is right at the time.

The teacher did not understand anxiety because she could not see it. It is what we call an invisible disability, and it is harder for people to understand because, on the outside, the child looks well, but on the inside, the child is suffering much fear and tension.

The teacher was utilizing a form of red light, yellow light, and green light. If the students stayed on green for the whole week, they got a special prize. For children with anxiety, this is one of the worst behavior management tools. The child spends the week worrying about staying on the green light. Imagine the stress this causes for the child, especially when they are trying and cannot live up to the unreasonable expectations. To expect a second grader to make no mistakes in the period of one week is unreasonable. Penalizing her for going to the restroom to cry because she was frustrated in the classroom should be a signal to change the system, not punish the child.

When Rachel learned Rose was going to the bathroom too much, Rachel feared that she might have diabetes. Recognizing this, Rachel made an appointment with the physician. That situation brought more stress for Rose when she had to get a urine sample and it was becoming even more apparent to Rachel that her daughter had anxiety. Rachel immediately came up with an alternative plan for her daughter. Throughout this whole stressful situation, Rachel showed empathy and understanding for her daughter.

By this time, you are seeing that Rachel was taking advice to learn as much as possible to find out what was going on with her daughter. It was very beneficial that she had a thorough evaluation done to see what challenges Rose was facing.

Rachel found out that her daughter had co-morbid needs (more than 1–2 different conditions) and that she would need a comprehensive approach to ensure Rose's needs were met.

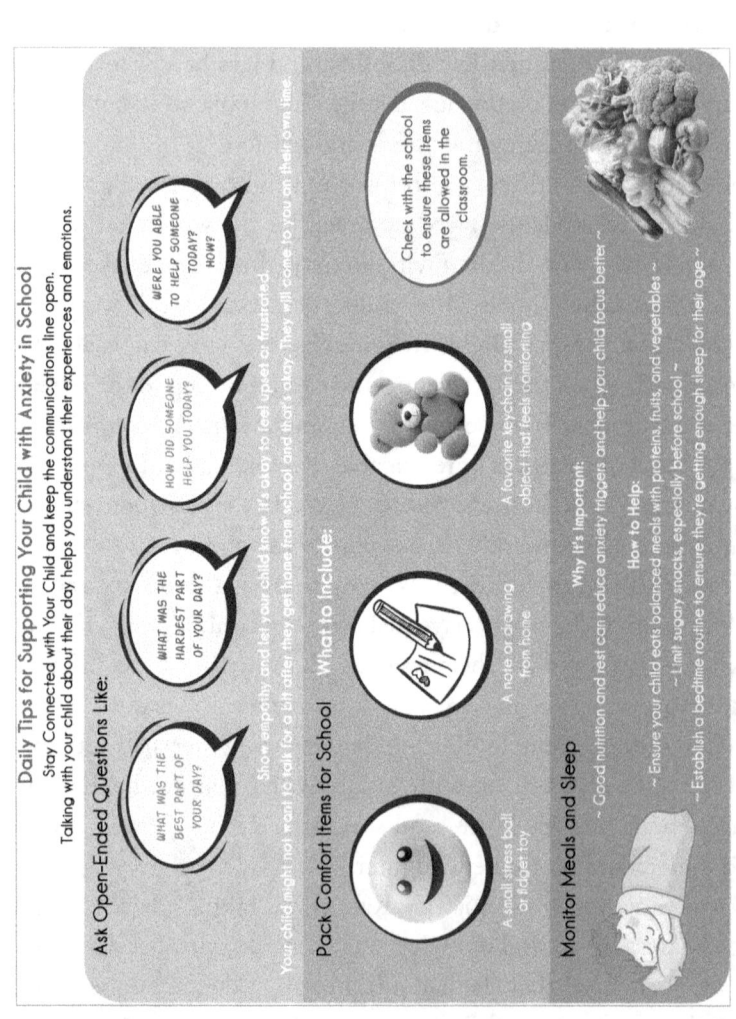

Figure 3.1
Daily tips for supporting your child with anxiety in school.
Nick Manker at Production Xpress

Takeaways

1. Be aware when teachers are utilizing a behavior management system that causes anxiety for children.
2. Do check out possible medical reasons that the child may be engaging in behaviors such as going to the restroom too much.
3. Think ahead to situations that might cause your child to have anxiety, and come up with alternative plans.
4. When securing an independent evaluation, make sure it is thorough and addresses all your child's needs.

Chapter 4
What's a 504 Plan?

Rachel's Story

I had met Rose's third grade teacher the year before and had heard great things about her teaching style. I was told that she was very caring and supportive of her students from a parent whose child she taught years before. Knowing that Rose would be in that type of environment helped ease my anxiety.

Third grade was in full swing, when Rose's teacher mentioned we needed to have a 504 meeting. It was not clear to me what a 504 meeting was or why it was needed. I had never heard of anything like this, and I was not sure how to prepare for it. Her teacher told me to expect a phone call and some paperwork would be coming home with Rose. I was hopeful there would be more of an explanation of what the meeting would entail, but that was not the case.

The notice arrived inviting me to the counselor's conference room on a set day and time. As a parent, my priority was to do what was best for Rose, but I felt uncertain and unprepared without knowing what a 504 plan was. I decided to research and learn more about what it meant. After a couple of quick internet searches, I discovered it was related to providing accommodations for Rose and the way she learns. I shared this information with my husband and we both agreed this would be beneficial for her.

The day arrived for the 504 meeting at the elementary school. I walked down the hallway and into a large conference room and recognized some of the people, and others I did not. I sat down at the table, feeling nervous as I did not understand why we needed to have this meeting.

Once the meeting started, a large screen displayed documents related to Rose and her education. This was also the first time I had heard the term "special education." The team went page by page discussing how she was doing in each subject. Throughout the meeting I was not asked any questions or given much of an opportunity to contribute. I felt like an outsider in a conversation about my own child. At the end of the meeting, I was handed a piece of paper and asked to sign it. I still had no clear understanding of what transpired in the meeting or what it would mean for Rose moving forward.

I signed the document because I trusted that the people in the room knew what was best for Rose, but inside, I felt a mix of confusion and frustration. I had hoped for more clarification and understanding of how this new plan would help Rose in the classroom. Instead, I left the meeting feeling overwhelmed. I had no idea about what steps would follow and whether the plan truly addressed Rose's needs. I knew I needed to educate myself on 504 plans, so I could be more involved in helping my daughter with her educational needs.

It would have been incredibly helpful to have someone to talk to about what our family was going through—whether it be another parent who had been through the same situation or a school staff member who could explain the process step by step. I had no idea what to do next, and the lack of guidance left me feeling alone and uncertain. I kept thinking how beneficial it would have been to have someone walk me through the details, answer my questions, and help me feel more confident about the plan being put in place for Rose.

This experience helped me understand that I needed to learn everything I could about special education. I knew this was something I needed to do to help Rose. I could not rely on anyone else to help me find the answers I was seeking. We wanted to ensure that she had every opportunity to succeed. I started reading, and researching everything I could to learn more about this new world we were thrust into. The goal was to empower myself so I could be a stronger advocate for Rose and ensure that her educational needs were truly being met.

After a few days, Rose brought home a large envelope. Inside was a copy of the 504 paperwork from the meeting and it had more information. As I read through everything, I noticed the ADHD box was checked and the "other" box was also checked for CAPD. It stated that her learning was substantially limited and that she qualified under section 504. Again, I still had no idea what that meant. I was assured that having this meeting and her qualifying would get her the help she needed in school. I also read that she would have "classroom modifications," which included extended time, re-teaching as needed, preferential seating, and an FM station tower. I also noticed her anxiety was not addressed in the meeting or on any of the paperwork. Anxiety was listed as one of her diagnoses, and there was no mention of it anywhere. Why were they not listing ways to support her emotionally?

A few weeks later, I received another meeting invite for an ARD (Navigate Life Texas), in which ARD stands for "admission, review, and dismissal." I had no idea what this meeting was for, and no one had explained it to me beforehand. The lack of communication left me feeling upset and overwhelmed. I realized that advocating for Rose was going to be a journey. I needed to learn and understand the system to better support Rose. I was forced into a complicated process without the necessary tools to navigate effectively.

This was a whole new world that I did not know much about. Why did no one from the school reach out to me and explain this process in a way that I could understand? It would have been extremely helpful to have a guide that broke down each step and gave me a sense of what to expect. As a parent, I was expected to advocate for my child, but I felt ill-equipped to do so without a better understanding of what I needed to do. I vowed to take more initiative in educating myself so I could be a voice for Rose. I could not help but feel frustrated that the support I needed was not more readily available.

The day came for the scheduled meeting. I once again walked into the same room as last time, but now it was called the ARD room. The same people that were at the first meeting were also there. I was quickly seated at the table, feeling a bit more prepared this time, though still unsure of what to expect. Once again, I sat quietly as they discussed Rose and her goals for the upcoming year. It felt as though the conversation was happening around me, and I was still trying to catch up with the process.

I heard a term that had not been mentioned before, an IEP (individualized education plan) and how having that plan in place would help Rose. I needed more clarification of what it entailed. Someone on the team gave me an explanation saying an IEP would give Rose more structure along with specific goals, modifications and accommodations tailored to her. I still felt a bit overwhelmed by the technical language and the number of people involved, some of whom I had never seen before.

The members of the ARD team spoke at length about developing new goals and whether Rose still needed support while at school. They discussed accommodations and modifications, but I still had no idea what they were talking about. I wanted to ask more questions, but I wasn't sure if I was able to be part of the conversation. No one at the table asked me for my thoughts or to chime in so I stayed quiet. I really wanted to fully understand how all of this would help Rose and what they were talking about would help her in the classroom. Although I did not understand what they were saying, I was grateful that Rose's needs were being taken seriously and that the team was working to develop a plan to support her. I could not help but wish there had been more guidance and clearer communication to help me fully understand the process.

This meeting lasted much longer than the last one as they had to review the assessment reports, and I noticed they had "Other Health Impairment" listed as needing to be monitored (see https://prntexas.org/other-health-impairment-ohi). It was another term I had not heard before, and I could not help but wonder what it really meant for Rose. I sat and listened as they went around the table, sharing their individualized reports of her. It felt like a blur, as each person spoke about their findings and the data they had collected.

I watched as the documents were being displayed on the large screen in front of me. They were using terms I had not heard of and what they were discussing was over my head. I could pick up bits and pieces, but most of the terminology was unfamiliar to me, and I felt like I was missing the bigger picture. Yes, they would talk to me and try to help me understand, but I was overwhelmed. I was not fully grasping the details of what was being presented. I wanted to speak on Rose's behalf, but the complexity of the process left me feeling uncertain about what to ask or how to engage more in these conversations. It would have been helpful to have someone to help me comprehend the full scope of the assessment and how each part of the plan would benefit Rose.

The meeting lasted about 45 minutes, and I was still not sure what the outcome was as there were many side conversations that I was not part of. I was asked to sign forms and handed a massive pile of papers—documents that seemed to hold the key to Rose's educational path. "Hang on to these," the coordinator advised, "you might need to reference them in the future."

I walked out of the meeting, with a mound of paperwork, and I was not sure what to do with what I had been given. I would have liked it if someone would have told me exactly what I needed to do next. I felt so lost. The lack of clear explanations during and after the meeting left me frustrated. Despite feeling that way, I was determined to learn everything I could and advocate for Rose's educational needs.

What's A Parent To Do?

It is clear from Rachel's story of her experience that educational personnel were not explaining the purpose of these meetings and were not giving Rachel time to ask questions. They were not seeking her input. They were using a lot of jargon without explaining any of it. The idea of the IEP being a collaborative process was not in place.

She was not told what a 504 plan was and when the 504 plan was created it did not address Rose's anxiety which is a disability that impacts a major life function which -- school.

It is unclear why they had an evaluation document created first and then came back together to do another meeting that was the IEP meeting. Some school districts combine the two and call it an MDC (multi-disciplinary conference). It is supposed to be a collaborative process for all involved, including the parent. Required participants are to be the general education teacher, the special education teacher, the parent, the student where appropriate, someone who can commit services, and someone who can interpret the results of the evaluation.

This narrative points to the fact that these meetings and they are called different names depending on what state you are located in, can be overwhelming to a parent for the first time, especially when there is no effort to make the parent feel they are an active participant at the time.

Notice is also to be given to the parent that they can bring someone with them. Oftentimes the parent is so busy processing all the terms that are being thrown at them that they miss part of the conversation so having someone else there can be very helpful. Parents may want to seek out an advocate who can help them through the process.

Many school districts have someone that is assigned to be the liaison with the parent. That individual is one who welcomes the parent and makes the parent feel like they are an integral part of the team.

Table 4.1
Your IEP roadmap.

Action	Why it matters
Establish the purpose of the meeting	Knowing the purpose of meetings ensures that you can actively participate and ask relevant questions. If the purpose isn't clear, request clarification and time to ask questions.
Request clear communication	Clear communication ensures that you are sufficiently informed. Jargon can be confusing and hinder understanding so don't be afraid to ask for terms to be explained in plain language.

(Continued)

Table 4.1
(Continued)

Action	Why it matters
Know your rights	The IEP process is collaborative, and parents have a critical role. Advocate for your role as an active participant and familiarize yourself with the IEP process in advance of the meeting. Detailed information about IDEA, including parents' rights, procedural safeguards and the IEP process can be found at your local Parent Training and Information Center website.
Bring support to the meeting	Having someone else present can help process information and ensure nothing is missed. Bring a trusted friend, family member, or advocate to meetings as they can help process information that might be missed due to being overwhelmed.
Connect with the special education coordinator	Special education coordinators encompass everything related to special education. Ask if your school district has a special education coordinator and if so, building a relationship with the coordinator can help you feel welcomed and integral to the team, a key element in fostering collaboration.

Takeaways

1. Seek out an advocate from the Parent Information and Training Center in your state. These individuals can attend IEPs and can help you navigate the process and better understand the terms.
2. Try to read as much in advance as you can about the special education process and do so before you go to the meeting.
3. If you believe you need more time to process the information being given to you at the meeting, ask for a copy of the reports and ask for a recess to give you time to study the information.

Chapter 5
From 504 to an IEP

Rachel's Story

Rose had two fantastic teachers for fifth grade; a main teacher and a co-teacher. Her co-teacher would pull her out of class when Rose needed extra time on an assignment. They were wonderful with her, and gave her the love and support she needed to excel. I appreciated both of them so much and they both became true friends.

Rose's time in elementary school was coming to a close, and it was hard to believe she was going to middle school. She had been doing well with the plans that had been in place for the last year, and it was time for another meeting about her individualized education program (IEP).

While I stood in the hallway, gearing up to meet with the ARD team, Rose's teacher and co-teacher pulled me aside and said, "Hey, before you go in there, ask for a REED (Review of Existing Evaluation Data). It's important to see if Rose needs any more assessments and to set her up for support as she heads into middle school next year."

I was taken aback but grateful for their guidance. I had no idea what a REED was, and hearing it from Rose's teachers felt like the first time someone was giving me specific advice on how to advocate for her in these meetings. They explained to me what a REED was, and that it would help determine if any additional evaluations were needed. It would ensure that Rose's IEP was updated to reflect any new needs or accommodations when she started middle school. I finally felt like I was being heard. Someone was giving me clear directions on what to do next. I felt a sense of relief as I had been struggling to keep afloat for the past couple of years. They must have seen the look on my face as I was about to enter another meeting that I was not prepared for. I appreciated them sharing their knowledge and offering me practical advice and it made me feel more prepared for the ARD.

In the meeting the ARD team concluded Rose would need a REED, and they actually scheduled it right then and there. I was so thankful for her teachers offering that suggestion as it was exactly what she needed to prepare for sixth grade.

A couple of weeks later, the school psychologist conducted the REED, and it was concluded that Rose needed to continue with the accommodations and modifications, which would continue through middle school. I felt a sense of relief that everything would still be in place to support her, and we could continue building on what was working for her. I signed another document, and they handed me what looked like a book. It was another mound of paperwork, filled with details about Rose's IEP and the modifications she would continue to receive. As they stated in our previous meetings, I was told to keep track of these papers, as they were important for Rose's school records and would serve as a reference for any future meetings.

What's a Parent To Do?

Parents know their children better than anyone and should trust their instincts when they sense their child is not progressing as well as they should. In this story, Rachel takes on much of the responsibility herself, and fortunately, Rose had an excellent advocate in her mother. Her mother knew Rose was struggling from the start when speech and language problems appeared. She also knew the importance of pursuing help for her child at an early age. Rachel pursued a speech and language evaluation, but that evaluation missed the language issues that Rose exhibited.

Under federal law, the school district has a responsibility to engage in "child find." The school district's job is to set up screenings throughout its geographic area where parents can bring their children. The advertisement for this should be widely disseminated so that all parents are aware of it. Rachel, a very active and knowledgeable parent, was informed that she had rights as a parent of a child suspected of having a disability. She did not know she had a right to have an evaluation completed by the school district because they suspected she had a disability. After learning of the free testing, Rachel had her child tested by a district-approved school psychologist.

Rachel did keep good records about what was happening and that is a must. Keep samples of your child's work and keep a log of when and to whom you talked in the school district and what they said to you. Everything should be in writing and should be dated and signed and you should also keep a copy.

Feeling overwhelmed and frustrated, Rachel didn't realize that there were advocates who could help her navigate the maze — and sometimes, the brick wall — she faced on her own. Rachel knew something was not right with the process that the school district was utilizing but she persisted and learned about the complexity of the system. Many parents just give up; they feel frustrated. Hopefully, an important lesson you learned from Rachel is that she was persistent, she visited the school frequently, and she knew that her daughter was not doing well. Parents have to be persistent, know their rights, and document what is happening in writing.

Figure 5.1
When your child is showing signs of a problem at an early age (sticky notes).

Nick Manker at Production Xpress

Takeaways

1. Seek out external support for you such as support groups, organizations that can give you support, and friends and families who may share a common experience. You need to know you are not alone.

2. Always put requests to the school district in writing, keep a copy, and send to several school personnel in case someone loses your request. Date and sign all requests.

Chapter 6
Middle School Challenges

Rachel's Story

The time for Rose to start middle school was quickly approaching. I reached out to one of the teachers who helped me in the last ARD meeting at her elementary school. I was a bit anxious about how Rose would handle the more demanding schedule and having to change classrooms every hour. Would it be too overwhelming for her with a more rigorous schedule than she was used to in elementary school? I felt reassured as she told me that kids like Rose often thrive in this kind of environment. It was very comforting to hear, and it eased my anxiety. It helped me feel more prepared for her move to middle school.

My husband and I were grateful for Rose's fifth grade teachers, and that they understood what her strengths and challenges were. It would help make it easier for her for the upcoming school year. This was going to be a big step for her, but hearing their perspective gave us confidence. I felt like we were entering this new chapter with the accommodations and modifications Rose would need in her classes. I was optimistic that she would continue to receive the support and guidance going forward. It was not going to be without its hurdles, but I was starting to believe that this next phase could be an opportunity for Rose to thrive.

On the first day of middle school, I could not tell who was more nervous, Rose or me. She was excited and ready to spread her wings, and eager to embrace her independence. I drove her to school, and all I could think about was I hoped she would have a fantastic year in her new school.

As we approached the area for drop-offs, I wasn't sure if Rose wanted me to walk her in or drop her off. She asked me to park the car and walk her to the front steps. I could see the excitement on her face. We walked to the front of the school, hugged each other goodbye, and Rose headed off to begin her next chapter.

The first few days of sixth grade were what I had expected. Rose was feeling a little overwhelmed by the chaos of having many different classes and navigating the new schedule. It was a big adjustment for her, but I tried to stay patient, knowing it would take time. I can only imagine, as it was a lot for any new student attending a new school. With figuring out different routines of having to change classes every hour, getting used to a school bell system that only allowed for five minutes to get to their lockers, and having multiple buildings to get to for a class, it was overwhelming for anyone.

After two weeks of Rose being in middle school, I had not met the Special Education Coordinator (SPED). I did not know their name or where their office was located. I thought since we had Rose's last IEP at her elementary school, then maybe we did not need to have another meeting until the end of the year? I still found it odd that I did not have a meeting with the SPED Coordinator to ensure each of Rose's teachers had her IEP.

A month passed, and I still had not met the SPED Coordinator. I did not even know who her counselor was or that I should have met with them to discuss her IEP plan. It was not until Rose started struggling in some of her classes that I realized something needed to be done. I asked around one of her teachers who I should talk to about getting her some extra help.

After another two weeks of waiting, the school psychologist finally referred me to the SPED Coordinator. I understood it can take time to get meetings scheduled especially for kids in the special education system. Although it had taken too long to make this connection, I was happy to meet them and get the process started to help Rose have her modifications and accommodations in place.

I made an appointment to see the Special Education Coordinator and was pleasantly surprised that she knew about Rose. On the other hand, I was also upset that she had not contacted me to set up a meeting. We talked about Rose having accommodations put in place to help her be successful in her classes. We decided to stay in touch via email or phone and meet whenever we felt it was necessary. I felt she had Rose's best interest at heart, and it made me feel better knowing that she would check in on her and ensure the teachers were following her IEP plan.

We reached October and Rose was still struggling with her schoolwork. Her anxiety was at an all time high. She would ask me daily to pick her up early from school. I tried my best to calm her fears and I reached out to her teachers, but frustratingly, I did not get any responses. I was desperate to try to help Rose, so I followed up with the SPED Coordinator, who I'd been meeting with regularly since the school year started.

I confided in her that my husband and I had discussed homeschooling Rose. I asked for her honest opinion, and to my surprise, she agreed that it might be the best option. She explained that many kids like Rose were slipping through the cracks in the education system, though Rose was fortunate because of mine and my husband's active involvement in her education. Hearing this broke my heart. How many kids were out there struggling without the support they needed?

It was a wake up call that made me think about the fairness of the school system and the challenges so many families like ours face.

It also reminded me how important it was for me to be the best advocate I could be for Rose. I wanted to ensure she had the best possible chance to succeed. The thought of homeschooling seemed overwhelming at first, but thinking about Rose thriving in an environment she would be comfortable in was worth considering. Was this something my husband and I would be able to take on? Of course, we would discuss this with Rose, as this would be something that would greatly affect her. This conversation left us determined to explore all options and make the best decision for Rose.

Rose was reluctant to leave her school, and her friends, but agreed to homeschool. I wanted her to be as involved as possible in her education, and let her choose subjects she wanted to learn more about. So, we headed off to the store that sold items for educators, and it was perfect for what we were looking for.

I bought every supply you could think of to make sure I was prepared to be my daughter's full-time teacher. Flashcards, books, art supplies—you name it, I got it. I even included Rose in the process, letting her pick out items she was most excited about. We spent hours at Lakeshore Learning Store, and I got to know the staff there so well that we were on a first-name basis! It felt good to dive into this new adventure together, making sure Rose had everything she needed to enjoy learning at home.

I made sure our first week of homeschooling was a time to unschool as we were not bound by any schedules. I wanted to keep it light and for us to find our rhythm together. At first, we did not have a set schedule as we were still figuring out this new adventure. I asked Rose about what she wanted to learn, and from there, I created lesson plans. I focused on teaching her the core subjects, but I also wanted to focus on topics she was interested in.

After a few weeks, we finally got into our new routine of homeschooling. Rose was more at ease, more willing to do her schoolwork, and seemed happier overall. I would let her decide where to go for a field trip and make the trip an educational one. We visited the Alamo because she, like her parents, was interested in history. Going to the bookstore, having lunch, and finding new places to work on her assignments positively affected her and it showed in her grades. I was not sure how long we would continue to educate her at home, but I knew that my husband and I were committed to do so for as long as she needed.

One spring afternoon, I met some friends for lunch when one of them asked me how Rose was doing. I told her that she was doing well with her studies, but I know she missed her friends. She told me that a new school was opening in the fall, and that she had done some research on it. My friend said the school would have small class sizes, be in a single building, and have an athletic program. I did not know much about a charter school or how they operate, but I was intrigued with what she shared. She told me about the schools educational approach and she thought it would be tailored to Rose's learning style. I was skeptical as it sounded too good to be true. I decided to look into it further, and see if this would be an option for Rose in the fall. The idea of her being in an environment where she could thrive both academically and athletically felt like a dream come true. Having an athletic program was a bonus as Rose was involved in year-round club swimming.

I researched the new school and learned it was a charter school. I had not even heard of a charter school, so that piqued my interest even more. I tried to find out more about how they teach children and how they would be able to help a struggling learner like Rose. Once again I was assured that this was *the* school for her to attend and that I should apply as soon as possible. After talking it over with my husband, we decided to give it a try, and if she got in, we could reassess Rose's school options.

Two weeks later, the day I had been waiting for finally arrived- the day to apply to the new school! I set my alarm and made sure I was ready by 6:00 a.m. when the registration portal opened. As I sat at my computer, I still was not 100% sure this was the perfect school for Rose, but I felt hopeful. I reminded myself that we had options if it did not work out. After submitting her application, I felt a mix of excitement and nerves, knowing this could be the start of a new chapter for Rose.

I was able to get Rose on the waitlist for the upcoming school year, and we were excited about this new opportunity. While that did not mean she was accepted, we were happy that there was a chance for her to possibly be a student in the fall.

One important fact that I learned was the school required uniforms. I was not sure how Rose would feel having to wear a button-down white shirt, plaid skirt, and knee-high socks. I thought to myself that this was a throwback to simpler times from the 1950s. She had to wear a uniform at her old middle school, which consisted of khaki pants and a school spirit shirt. To my surprise, she was not bothered with her new required wardrobe; it also made mornings a lot easier getting ready when she knew what she would be wearing every day.

A few weeks later, we got the call that Rose had been accepted for the Fall. It was time to make a decision on where she would attend school for the upcoming year. We talked it over as a family, and Rose decided she wanted to give the charter school a try. I was a little reluctant as the school did not offer an open house, so I could not prepare Rose for her first day. There was not an opportunity to meet the teachers or tour the building where she would be spending the majority of her days. But we still felt like this was a great opportunity for Rose and we had high hopes this was the right place for her to be.

What's a Parent to Do?

Rachel had tried to work with the school and was feeling overwhelmed and reached the point that she needed to look for other options for her daughter. The school's SPED Coordinator should have worked with Rachel to pursue other options within the school. It was unfortunate that the coordinator wanted Rose to leave the school. Schools have a moral and legal responsibility to find the most appropriate options within their school. Their obligation is to serve all the children within their district. However Rachel did make the decision that she thought was best for her daughter. In the homeschool option she focused on Rose's strengths and what Rose desired to learn and was motivated to learn. Rachel then realized this might not be the most appropriate option for Rose so then she did her homework and found another placement for her daughter.

Table 6.1
Your roadmap for navigating challenges

Action	Why it's important
Collaborate with school staff	Schools have a moral and legal obligation to serve all children within their district. Coordinators should work with you to explore all options within the school before considering alternatives.
Focus on your child's strengths	Highlighting a child's strengths and interests can boost motivation and engagement in learning.
Advocate for your child's needs	Ensure the school is actively seeking appropriate solutions for your child's education.
Evaluate alternative options thoughtfully	If the current school placement isn't working, carefully researching and evaluating other educational options may help you find your child's best fit.
Make decisions based on your child's best interests	Prioritize your child's needs, strengths, and well-being when making educational decisions, even if it means pursuing non-traditional paths.

Takeaways

1. Recognize that moving to middle school may be difficult because the child is experiencing multiple teachers, more students, and multiple classes, and at the same time your child is experiencing hormonal changes.

2. Familiarize yourself with all the teachers your child will have before classes start.

3. Identify a point person who you can contact when there is a problem.

Chapter 7

The Charter School Experience

Rachel's Story

The day had finally arrived for Rose to start her seventh-grade year at the new charter school. She wanted to ride the bus to school for her first day, and I was a little sad that I was not going to be taking her for the first time ever! Since the school was thirty minutes away, they offered a charter van to pick the kids up in our neighborhood. My husband and I were not sure if we wanted to pay the monthly fee of $250, but since we both worked, it was the best choice for us.

The day flew by and it was time to pick her up. I went to the van drop off location at precisely 3:05 p.m. and I was excited for Rose, and to hear how much she enjoyed her new school. But when she got in the car, she started describing her "school," and my excitement quickly faded. It turned out her school was in the basement of a church. There was a single hallway with five classrooms—none of them had windows. The teachers did not even have their own dedicated classrooms; they rotated between rooms depending on the grade they were teaching. It was not at all what I had pictured, but I knew we needed to give it a chance for Rose's sake.

DOI: 10.4324/9781003629313-7

There were plenty of adjustments for all of us. The new routines, the different expectations, and not knowing anyone, all felt a bit overwhelming. Naturally, I found a way to get involved and help us all settle in. I joined forces with other new parents to start the parent–teacher organization (PTO). Being part of the PTO was incredibly helpful. It gave the families a chance to connect with each other, share experiences, and lean on one another as we navigated this new journey together. Since it was the first charter school campus in San Antonio, we were all in the same boat, figuring things out as we went along. It was reassuring to know we had a supportive community backing us up.

I was surprised by the school's curriculum as it was not at all what we expected. Students were not allowed to read books published after 1950 or discuss anything related to pop culture, which seemed odd to me. On top of that, all students were required to take Latin, a language neither my husband nor I were familiar with. What had we gotten ourselves into with this school?

Another issue that concerned me was that after three weeks at the new school, I still had not been contacted about scheduling an ARD (or IEP, as most states call it) meeting to put Rose's plan in place for the school year. When I spoke with one of her teachers, they had not even heard that she had an IEP. This was troubling because all her teachers should have known about it from the beginning. I reached out to the SPED Coordinator to set up a meeting. I wanted to make sure that all of Rose's teachers had a copy of her IEP and they were fully aware of her accommodations and modifications she was supposed to receive. I was frustrated and felt like we were starting from scratch, but I knew I had to advocate for Rose to ensure she got the support she deserved.

The day finally came after weeks of Rose being in school, for me to meet with the SPED Coordinator, and the rest of the people who would help Rose while she was at school. I was looking forward to connecting with the team that would help Rose have a successful year at her new charter school. When I walked into what I thought was his office, I found myself in an old classroom instead. He was the only one there. "Where's the team?" I asked, genuinely confused. He looked at me with a look of panic, clearly having no idea what I was talking about. My heart sank, and I could not help but ask how many of these meetings he had actually presided over. He admitted that he had never conducted an ARD or an IEP meeting before. How could this school claim to support kids who learn differently if their SPED Coordinator had never even participated in an ARD? Despite my doubts, I presented Rose's previous IEP and explained how she learned best. I could not believe I had to explain all this to someone who is in the special education world. He assured me he would get Rose's IEP to her teachers, but I felt uneasy at his lack of experience. I did not want to ruin Rose's excitement about her new school, as she seemed so happy in her new environment. I still had my reservations about the school's ability to meet her needs, but my husband and I decided to give them time to get her supports and accommodations in place.

Rose came home the next day, and I asked if any of her teachers had spoken to her about her IEP. She said they had not. Deciding to give it a bit more time, I hoped the SPED Coordinator would soon alert her teachers about her plan. I also did not want to worry her, but I felt myself becoming increasingly upset.

The following week, Rose came home and showed me that she had received a demerit and that meant she needed to serve detention. "A demerit? What in the world for?" I asked. She handed me the paper and explained that she needed to serve detention because she did not have a button on the back of her pants pocket. I stared at the note, baffled. How was this real? Was the school really punishing kids for something so trivial?

Rose could not believe that she was in trouble for something as ridiculous as this. What kind of school had I enrolled her in that this would warrant an infraction? Was this their idea of teaching discipline to their students? Why would they penalize a child over something as minor as a missing button? The school's philosophy and their promises of a supportive environment were what they were known for in Arizona, but this made me question whether their priorities were truly in the right place.

I picked Rose up from detention and asked her what they had to do after school for their punishment. She told me they had to place their hands flat on a desk and sit up straight for thirty minutes. They were not allowed to talk, move, or even adjust their hands for the entire 30 minutes. My husband and I were shocked. It seemed to us like they were running a military training camp rather than a school focused on educating kids.

Our hopes for this school being the one we thought would best suit Rose were quickly fading with each passing day. It seemed every day brought a new reason to doubt our decision to enroll her in this new school. Despite Rose's happiness, we could not shake the feeling that this might not be the supportive, nurturing environment she needed.

Two weeks later, Rose came home with another demerit, and I was stunned, as this one left my husband and I completely floored. The school conducted monthly fire drills, and on this particular day, it was raining. Despite the weather, the students were required to go outside. While waiting for the all-clear to re-enter the building, Rose slipped and made a noise as she fell. She quickly got back up and rejoined her classmates as they returned to their classroom. However, once inside, her teacher pulled her aside and issued her a demerit for "making a noise during the fire drill." Once again, Rose served her 30 minutes of detention sitting completely still and silent with hands face down on her desk.

Another week passed, and Rose still had not been approached about her IEP from any of her teachers. While I wanted to give her the chance to advocate for herself, it became clear that it was time for me to step in. No one had reached out to her or me, so I decided to contact her teachers directly to see if they had received her IEP. To my disbelief, not only had they not received her IEP, but they did not even know what an IEP was. How could they be certified teachers as surely they learned about that in one of their college courses? I decided to look further into the school's policies, and I learned that teachers at a charter school were not required to be certified. I also learned this was common in charter and private schools, but I was shocked to realize that many of Rose's teachers were new to teaching. For some, this was their first teaching job, and they had minimal experience in a classroom setting.

As the weeks went by, Rose started to complain that her stomach hurt while she was at school and began asking me to pick her up early. I recognized the pattern as a sign that her anxiety was rearing its ugly head. It broke my heart to see her suffer, but my husband and I knew this school was not meeting her needs or supporting her in the way she needed. It became evident that the charter school was not the right fit for her.

Once again we had another conversation with Rose to discuss her options on where to go to school. We discussed the pros and cons of staying at the same school, homeschooling or going back to her previous middle school. It was important to make sure that Rose had a say in what she wanted to do and not just her dad and I making that decision for her.

In February, we made the difficult decision to unenroll her, as she decided she would go back to homeschooling. Saying goodbye to the friends we made while at that school was bittersweet, but we knew it was the best choice for Rose. While she was not thrilled about the idea of homeschooling for her final year before high school, we felt it might be the best path forward to avoid repeating the challenges she faced previously.

We took a few weeks off to decompress, and give Rose time to unschool as we had done in the past. It was a much needed reset for all of us. It also gave her mind a break from the rigorous academics she experienced at the charter school. Her anxiety had intensified during her last weeks at school, and I knew we both needed time to unwind and regain perspective. I wanted Rose to have some downtime and for us to explore learning in a more relaxed environment. While we would continue teaching the core subjects, I wanted her to choose topics she would find interest in learning. As we had previous experience with homeschooling, I already had ideas for what she would want to study. She enjoyed going on trips to museums, nature hikes, and doing creative projects at home. This also gave me time to come up with some lesson plans and consider what would best support Rose. I wanted her to feel included in her learning journey and for us to figure out a schedule that did not feel too confined. Taking this break was a big decision and it allowed us to recharge and refocus on what truly mattered and that was Rose's happiness.

There were only three months left of the school year, so I decided we would focus on making learning enjoyable and not stick to a regular schedule. We also wanted Rose to learn about life skills like managing finances, budgeting, and even something as simple as writing a check. These skills are often not taught in a traditional school setting, but we felt it was essential for her to learn. Rose had faced many hurdles in her educational journey, but we were determined to make sure she had a well-rounded education that prepared her not just academically, but for life beyond school.

March was approaching and it was time to make the definitive choice about Rose's high school path. The decision needed to be made about whether she should continue homeschooling or transition to a smaller, more intimate school environment. One of the options was the high school, her older siblings had gone to. It had over 3,000 students, and the sheer size of it was a significant factor in our talks with Rose. We knew she needed to make the decision, but we also wanted her to know she had our full support. After discussing as a family and weighing various factors, Rose told us that she wanted to graduate from the same school as her older brother and sister. After considering our options, we agreed that it was the best fit for Rose. Making another change in schools was not easy for her. We wanted to make sure she felt confident and supported in her choice and that was the most important thing to us.

It had been a little over two years since Rose had seen anyone she went to public school with. I could not help but feel nervous about how she would be received by classmates she had not seen in a long time. During her time away from school, not a single one of her old "friends" had reached out to her, which added to my concern. Despite my anxiety, I reminded myself of how strong my daughter was with everything she had been through. Rose had faced challenges before and she faced them head on and always came out on top. Even if she did not always show it, I knew she had an inner strength that would guide her. I decided to focus on the possibility that this would be a fresh start for Rose, and a chance to reconnect with her old friends, and perhaps form new friendships. I believed she would find her way and be okay. One positive factor was that Rose's older sister, Alexis, would be a senior while she started as a freshman. Knowing they would be together helped ease my concerns. It felt like a positive situation for both my girls, offering them a chance to support each other through this new chapter of their lives.

What's a Parent to Do?

We must consider how stressful it was for Rachel to see that this charter school, for which she had high hopes, had very strange practices with little or no oversight. Rachel was torn. Her daughter seemed to be doing okay, but at the same time, she knew this program was not right for her.

At this point Rachel had experienced what Bev would define as "decision fatigue." Rachel was having to make so many decisions about what would be appropriate for her daughter. At the same time, she was faced with educators who either did not know about the law or chose to play a game that they did not know about the law.

Although the charter school may not have had fully credentialed teachers, it still had a responsibility to provide a "free appropriate public education" (FAPE) for Rose. The local school was responsible for the education of students with disabilities and is charged with overseeing what the charter school is doing unless the state is the entity that monitors the charter school. In any event, the charter school must provide special education services.

It is important to note that throughout this whole experience, Rachel was striving to develop the most appropriate curriculum and instruction for her daughter while also serving as a parent.

Through the middle school years, she continued her advocacy, never giving up. This is an important lesson for all parents. Rose was fortunate to have a parent who kept asking questions, challenging what was happening, and seeking solutions to the difficulties her daughter was facing.

Takeaways

1. Realize that being a parent of a child who has disabilities will require many years of advocacy. When you are advocating for your child with a disability you are also advocating and setting the path for all of those children who do not have a parent who can advocate for them.
2. Study the laws and regulations so you are informed about what can and cannot be done to help your child.
3. Be aware that you can experience decision fatigue and find a support group or an advocate to assist you.

Chapter 8
Pursuing Outlets for Anxiety

Rachel's Story

Before we knew it, It was time to enroll Rose for the fall semester. I gathered all of her paperwork and school documents, and we headed to the high school to register her. With two older children who had attended the same school, including one who had graduated, I had built a solid relationship with the guidance counselor. I felt reassured to know that all three of my children had the same counselor, and that helped alleviate some of my concerns. He knew I had three children and recalled meeting Rose previously. I had hoped the registration process would go smoothly, thanks to the binders where I meticulously kept all of Rose's documentation since our journey began many years ago.

One of Rose's biggest worries was who she would sit with at lunch. For a child with anxiety, finding a place to sit and someone they know they can sit with can be a major stressor. In elementary school, everyone eats together as a class, but in middle and high school, it's a different story. This was very important to Rose and was a big concern of hers. Rose, her counselor, and I strategically planned her schedule so she could eat lunch at the same time as her sister. Some might think this level of planning is excessive, but for Rose, it meant finding stability and support in a new environment. With a school of over 3,000 students, and three lunch periods, having at least 1,000 people have your exact lunch time can feel overwhelming.

During our discussions, the counselor mentioned that Rose would have a case manager to support her while in high school. This person would serve as her primary contact and be her advocate while at school. I had not heard of the role of "case manager," and I was surprised to learn that there were 27 case managers at the high school, each dedicated to supporting students like Rose. I felt more at ease that she would have the support she needed to navigate high school successfully and knowing she had someone to help advocate for her at school, was a relief. Her having a case manager and her sister also having the same lunch, reassured me that we were setting her up for a positive experience at her new school. As I walked out of the counselor's office, I felt a mix of emotions. I was nervous about the challenges ahead but also optimistic that we had taken the right steps to set Rose up for success.

Rose's passion for swimming had been a constant in her life, so it was natural that she wanted to try out for the high school swim team. Missing the spring tryouts turned out to be a blessing in disguise, as it gave her time to prepare for the August tryouts after taking a break from club swimming. Thankfully, she had the entire summer and the neighborhood swim team to help her regain her competitive edge. Rose was dedicated, and she practiced for hours every day. Watching Rose pursue this goal that she had set for herself years ago filled me with pride. It was not just about her making the team, but seeing her follow through on one of her long-time goals, and love for the sport.

Rose's anxiety about the swim team tryouts was at an all time high. I reached out to another Mom for advice whose daughter was already on the team. I asked her about what I needed to prepare Rose for during the tryout process. Should I talk to the coach about her anxiety? Was there a possibility for an individual tryout? The mom empathized with my concerns and promised to speak to the coach. reassuring us that Rose would be ready by August. Was that the right decision on my part to ask her to speak with the coach? I was not sure, but after watching Rose struggle for years, I just wanted something to go right for her. Making this team was so important to her and I decided it was worth it to ask her to speak to him.

The mom got back to me and told me that Rose would need to go through the tryout process just like everyone else. While it was not what I wanted to hear, it actually ended up being the right decision. This would inevitably push Rose out of her comfort zone, and sometimes that is a good thing. I told Rose and I let her know that she would need to go through the regular tryout process like the rest of the new swimmers. We discussed different ideas together to help her stay focused and prepare mentally. Despite my unwavering belief in her abilities, Rose was grappling with self-doubt, and my biggest fear was that she might consider not trying out at all.

The day that Rose had circled on her calendar and had thought about for years had finally arrived: time for the high school swim team tryouts. I drove her to the natatorium, kissed her forehead for luck, and made my way up to the stands, camera in hand. The tryouts proved to be very demanding, but Rose had prepared for how hard it was going to be. I watched nervously, uncertain if Rose would push through the challenges. My hands were shaking so much that I struggled to keep the camera steady. As Rose dove into the pool and began her tryout, I was amazed; she not only kept pace with the other swimmers, there also seemed to be a confidence about her with each stroke.

When Rose finished her final lap, she hopped out of the water, gathered her belongings and met me where I had dropped her off earlier. We both wished that we would find out while we were at the natatorium, but the coach still had more swimmers to evaluate. It would be a few days until we received word of whether she made it or not. I felt so much pride in Rose's performance that it was overwhelming. Seeing her determination and skill on display filled me with hope that she would achieve her goal of making the team.

After what felt like weeks of waiting to hear if she had made the team, we finally received the news that Rose had made it! We were all so elated, and so happy for her! Rose was beaming with happiness and we could not have been more proud of her for having the courage to face her fears. A thoughtful neighbor surprised Rose by putting up a congratulatory sign in our yard. It was so sweet of her to think of Rose and that made her feel even more special. This was a huge milestone that she had wanted to achieve and she did it!

Before the start of the school year, the Parent Teacher Association and the school organize something called "prep days." The purpose of this program is to assist students, particularly freshmen and new students, in obtaining their school books, signing up for clubs, receiving their schedules, and touring the campus. I had previously volunteered to work on those days in years past, so I understood what Rose would experience on her assigned day. However, the night before her scheduled prep day at the school, she had an anxiety attack. She was upset and saying that she did not want to go. She wanted me to gather her things for her and bring them home. She did not want to see anyone she knew or had gone to school with in the past. Rose never likes it when people ask her questions, particularly the big question "where have you been?" I knew that she was going to have to get used to seeing students that she had known for years, but I also wanted her to tour the school. The campus was very large, and she needed to find her classes.

Her sister Alexis and I convinced her to go to prep days and it helped that I volunteered on her assigned day so she could stop by and see me if she needed an escape. Alexis was going to be more helpful than anyone during Rose's first year of high school as the girls would be together for one year. We did not know just how much at the time.

The girls came to get Rose's schedule, and then Alexis proceeded to guide her through the rest of the tasks Rose needed to do to be prepared to start school. Later that day, Rose told me that she managed to avoid seeing or talking to anyone. She rushed through everything to finish quickly. She mentioned she did not stop by the spirit section to buy any school shirts, and asked me to go look for her. I knew she needed to do this on her own, but I also knew that her anxiety was at an all-time high as she got ready to start school.

What's A Parent to Do?

Throughout this book you have seen how Rachel recognized that it was important to build on Rose's strengths, so swimming was a wonderful outlet for Rose, but the competitiveness of trying out for the team provided more anxiety for Rose. Sometimes a parent has to weigh the efforts to make sure their child builds on their strengths. Once Rose had tried out, she could stay in the sport and do what she liked to do.

Rachel had such a positive relationship with her daughter that her daughter told her what caused her anxiety. As a parent, Rachel was a good listener and that is critical that a parent be in tune with the child's needs and was not judgmental or harsh with her daughter.

Table 8.1
Addressing challenges while supporting strengths

Action	Why it matters
Build on your child's strengths	Encouraging activities that align with your child's strengths can boost confidence and provide a positive outlet. However, it's important to balance this with an understanding of potential stressors (like competitiveness) to avoid overwhelming them.
Collaborate with the school	Brainstorming solutions with the school, such as addressing anxiety-inducing situations like lunchtime, ensures a supportive environment for your child.
Be a good listener	Listening without judgment or harshness will allow you to be in tune with your child's emotional and mental well-being, fostering trust and understanding. Maintaining an environment where your child feels comfortable sharing their concerns will help you understand and address your child's needs effectively.
Balance effort and well-being	Weighing the effort required for activities against their impact on your child's mental health ensures a healthy balance between growth and emotional stability.

Takeaways

1. Secondary schools can be large and very overwhelming for a child with anxiety—they worry they will get lost, will be late for class, will not know who they can sit by at lunch, and so on. Try to identify in advance possible problematic times and situations.

2. Once you identify with your child what those problem areas might be, develop a plan together with your child.

3. Identify who your child's case manager is prior to the start of the school year, then meet with the individual. Include your child in the visit so she knows who she can go to in the event of a crisis.

Chapter 9
The Complexity of Anxiety

Rachel's Story

It was time for Rose to start high school, and my husband and I had hoped this was the right decision. She had been through so much, that we both wanted her to have a successful year. I was not sure how the day would go for her, but I was happy knowing that her sister would be at the same school. Before they headed off for their senior and freshman years, I made sure to snap a picture just as I had done for every first day of school. I pulled Alexis aside and thanked her for being such a supportive big sister. My anxiety was lessened because I knew Rose would not be alone.

The girls came home and told me all about their first day of school. They were so excited, and that made my heart happy. Rose had not been excited about anything school-related in a long time. I could not help but wonder if this would be the year that would help Rose feel less anxious at school. I could only hope.

Rose had been in school for almost two weeks and I had not heard from anyone about having her IEP meeting. I contacted her counselor and asked what I needed to do to get that scheduled. He told me to contact the School Psychologist and see if a meeting had been set for Rose's ARD. I had no information on who that person was or what I was supposed to be doing to make this happen.

I searched on the school website to see if I could find the information for the school psychologist. I finally found the person I needed to contact and sent her an email. She asked if I had been contacted by her case manager, and I told her no, I had not. School had been in session for two weeks and even Rose did not know who she was. My frustration grew into anger. Had she given Rose's teachers her IEP? Do her teachers even know she had an IEP? While I understand case managers have a lot of kids they oversee, a quick email introducing themselves would have been nice. I did not understand how this continued to happen at every school she went to. If Rose was being overlooked, then how many other students was this happening to. Rose at least had an advocate in me, but I wondered how many of the kids with an IEP did not have their supports in place.

I soon learned the answer to my questions, as a teacher called upon Rose during class; that is a prime example of what is listed on her IEP for what not to do and not to call on her during class. I emailed the school psychologist and she told me we needed to schedule Rose's ARD. I thought that was something already being taken care of, but I was wrong.

The school psychologist let me know that we needed to have a meeting in order to address that particular accommodation. This confused me as it was listed in her IEP, but I can only guess that none of Rose's teachers had a copy of her accommodations and modifications. She also told me that she would forward my email regarding my concerns to her case manager.

Another couple of weeks come and go, and I still have not heard from the person who is supposed to be my child's point of contact while in school; her case manager. As it was explained to me, this person would advocate on Rose's behalf, and I have yet to find out who they are after weeks of Rose being in school.

The school psychologist once again tells me she let her case manager know that she needed to contact me as soon as possible and she has now looped in both of the Campus Coordinators. Who are they? Why am I just now hearing about this? Miraculously, once the case manager's boss was notified of her lack of communication, I received an email from her. I learned the case manager's name and looked up her profile on the school website. I needed a face with a name.

I finally felt like the train was moving forward, but once again, Rose was let down. After another two weeks go by, I still had not heard from the case manager, School Psychologist, or the Special Education Coordinator. Almost one month, of Rose not having her supports in place was concerning. I emailed all of Rose's teachers and sent them her IEP; they had no idea she even had an IEP. I was told once again that a meeting was going to be put on the schedule and that I would hear from her case manager as soon as possible. Amazingly enough, I heard from Ann (that was the case manager's name), and an ARD had been scheduled. Why did it take me jumping through hoops to get in touch with her and to set this meeting? It would take another two weeks for the meeting to take place.

Two more days go by, and I still have not heard anything about her ARD. My husband told me he received an email from the Special Education Clerk. Um, ok, who was that person, and why was she contacting him and not the both of us? Come to find out, they only had his contact information and not mine. I could not believe that as I had been emailing practically everyone in the Special Education Department, and they did not have my contact information.

What's a Parent to Do?

Rose has two invisible disabilities—anxiety and a learning disability—and it is hard for teachers, parents, and other students to understand that just because we cannot see the disability, that does not mean that the disability is not real. Rose and her mother were doing an outstanding job of coping with the trials and tribulations of working with individuals who did not have a grasp of Rose's individual needs and certainly did not understand the special education process.

We have learned here about the ripple effect of the learning disability and the anxiety. Rose was legitimately worried. Her needs were not being met at school. High school has multiple challenges for all students, especially for students who have anxiety and learning disabilities. Rachel was worried that Rose would not succeed, that she would not make the swim team and that she would not have friends in high school. Her sister helped and may have felt stress because of her overwhelming sense of responsibility. Alexis cared about her sister and wanted to make sure she was successful.

A parent once said it, and it is so true that with every milestone that a student faces, it is stressful for the parent, and the stages of grieving are once again activated. The parent feels first shock, then disbelief, denial, anger, bargaining, and finally acceptance. When a parent has a child who has a disability, parents go through a mourning process as they work through these stages. It is indeed a roller coaster of emotions. The emotions of the parent then impact the emotions of the child. Rose was going through a difficult time, Rachel was worried, and thus Rose was worried as they worked through this myriad of emotions that impacted the family. Rachel recognized that for Rose it would be difficult for her to find a place to sit for lunch and for Rose to try out for the swim team. Rachel walked the fine line between wanting independence for her daughter while at the same time, Rose's anxiety made it impossible for her to be alone in those decisions. Rose's sister, Alexis, was in the background supporting her and cheering her on. Rachel volunteered for prep days, so she knew what was expected.

As we read this, we learned that Rachel found a champion for Rose at school, the guidance counselor. That person was reliable and

Rachel felt he could be trusted. In the real world of some large schools, there are case managers but at times those individuals are assigned so many students to watch out for that the caseload is unmanageable. Rachel, as the parent, was persistent, and that is crucial.

Rose's anxiety was invisible and therefore many people had a difficult time understanding what she was going through. Her mother was the champion in building awareness.

Takeaways

1. Identify a point of contact person in your school who you believe is an advocate for your son or daughter.

2. When having your child tested, have your child evaluated by someone who will do a thorough job of examining whether there are co-morbidities in existence such as anxiety and depression or anxiety and learning disabilities. Co-morbidities are being found to be common in students with disabilities so we must thoroughly examine the complexities of the issues the child may be facing.

3. Understand that people have a more difficult time understanding the needs of children with disabilities that cannot be seen such as learning disabilities or anxiety. They may say, "The child looks normal to me," when in fact the child has an internal disability as opposed to an external one such as a physical disability that can be seen.

Chapter 10
Making Connections

Rachel's Story

Finally after what seemed like months, it was time for Rose's ARD, and I was feeling more nervous than usual. I could not believe that the high school was not more prepared. As I walked into the ARD, I noticed several new faces, except for her counselor, who had also been the contact for my two older kids while they were in school. Despite having been to numerous of these types of meetings, I felt inadequate. I knew I was prepared and I wanted everyone in that room to recognize that. For every school meeting regarding Rose, I always made sure to bring all the documentation that I had collected since she was three years old. I carried my binders, and I'm sure I looked quite intimidating, almost like a lawyer going to court! I wanted to be able to answer any questions and with all of the papers I had in my binders, I prepared.

In high school, they want the student to be in the ARD meeting as they feel like the student is old enough to understand what the meeting entails. Rose had sat in on an IEP meeting in elementary school, but had not been in one since. She does not like when people are talking about her while she is in the room. I prepared her for what the meeting would be about so she would feel a little bit more comfortable as they started their discussion. Knowing everyone would be talking about her while she was at the table made her uneasy, but she understood she needed to be there.

I sat in the ARD with Rose and listened to them talk about making sure all of her teachers had her IEP. Finally, after weeks of emails, and phone calls, I felt that everyone was on the same page and I felt good about the outcome. I was happy to finally meet Rose's case manager in person and to put a face to a name, and I know Rose was glad to see who she was, too. I was so happy that Rose had a point person other than her sister who could help guide her while in school.

The next week I picked Rose up from swim practice and she mentioned one of her teachers called on her again in class. She said it had happened a couple of times even though all of her teachers had her IEP. I started to get very upset as this was just discussed in our ARD the week before. I was told we needed to have the meeting to make sure all of her modifications and accommodations were in place. I decided to contact Ann and ask if she had given all of Rose's teachers her IEP. I also thought I would contact each of her teachers to see if they had a copy of her paperwork. I was shocked to discover that none of Rose's teachers had received her IEP, or even knew that she had one. Why does this keep happening? This was the main reason to have the ARD. Why had her case manager not shared her accommodations and modifications? I was really upset, and I'm sure Rose felt the same way.

That evening I emailed her case manager, and I hoped she would see my email the first thing in the morning when she got to school. But I never received a response. My frustration was mounting, yet I was still determined to ensure her IEP was being followed. After not hearing from her case manager yet again, emailing her and this time I also included the special education coordinator and the school psychologist, hoping for someone to get in touch with me. The lack of communication from anyone in the special education department was astonishing. Weeks passed with no resolution, and I found myself feeling increasingly isolated in my efforts to advocate for Rose. Why was it so difficult for someone to answer me?

I told Alexis how frustrated I was with Rose's case manager. Both of the girls had the same teachers for their foreign language class. Alexis told me their teachers asked how Rose was doing, and she told them about the situation with the case manager. One of the teachers told Alexis that Rose needed a case manager who would be supportive and would help her get the accommodations she needed. They had just the person in mind, Ms. Jones. I thought to myself, what would it hurt to get a new person who would actually go to bat for Rose, and be her advocate at school? So, I sent an email to the school counselor the next day, and lo and behold, I was able to get the case manager her teacher had recommended! I did not know anything about Ms. Jones, but the fact that two teachers said she was the case manager to have in your corner, made me so appreciate their recommendation.

Ms. Jones was the perfect person for Rose to have as an advocate. She emailed me almost daily to check in and see if I needed anything, and she often reached out to ask how Rose was doing at home. It was a night-and-day experience compared to what we had been through before. Having someone who genuinely cared about Rose, even calling after school hours, made all the difference. Knowing that Ms. Jones was there as a point person Rose could lean on at school was like having a heavy weight lifted off my shoulders. She went above and beyond, ensuring Rose felt supported and valued. I felt reassured every morning when I dropped her off at school. She finally had someone in who believed in her and would help advocate for her.

Rose had new accommodations in place, and the one that helped the most was the pass that Ms. Jones had created specifically for her. Whenever Rose felt anxious, she simply needed to show the pass to her teacher, no matter which class she was in. It was a small card that looked like a business card Rose could use when things became overwhelming if she is in a classroom. She did not need to go to the front of the class to the teachers desk to let her know she was leaving. It gave Rose a since of peace knowing she could stay in her chair and make sure the teacher saw the card.

This pass gave her permission to visit Ms. Jones in her room, which was a designated safe space that was always open to her.

Once in her room, Rose could take the time to take a break and reset before returning to her day. This simple accommodation became one of the most important things to Rose and it helped manage her anxiety. It helped her build the confidence to advocate for her own needs and feel more in control of her school experience.

Some days, Rose would not make it to any of her classes, instead Ms. Jones would let all of her teachers know that she was at school, and that she would be staying in her class for the day. Rose and Ms. Jones formed a wonderful connection and I considered her a friend. She would buy Rose lunch some days and they would sit in the quiet of her room and disconnect with the world. Ms. Jones was one of the main reasons Rose was able to stay in school until graduation, and for that, my husband and I were so appreciative of her.

Ms. Jones made sure that Rose was responsible for completing her work and staying in touch with her teachers to ensure she was not falling behind. She also stayed in contact with her teachers to make sure they followed Rose's IEP. I was so thankful for her dedication to making sure Rose received the support she needed at school. It gave me peace of mind, and I know it helped Rose as well.

Some days were not easy. A long weekend, Thanksgiving break, holiday break, and spring break were especially challenging for Rose. After each break, it was a struggle for her to transition back to the routine of school. Most of those times, Rose would miss anywhere from one to five days, needing extra time to prepare herself mentally and emotionally to return to her regular schedule.

I could only imagine how overwhelming it must have been for her to walk into a school with 3,000 students, and not feel anxious. Despite all of the challenges, Rose showed resilience in her own way. Even though it took time, and some weeks she would only make it two or three days, she always found the strength to get back to her schedule.

Her case manager and I had our routine on days when Rose did not feel 100%. We would discuss how many classes she would attend that day, whether it was just one or two. If she felt up to it, we would start with the first class, and I would wait in the car outside the school while she was in class. When she was ready, I'd drive to the back of the school to pick her up.

On the tougher days, I would often call on Ms. Jones, who was always willing to step in and try to help Rose feel supported. Sometimes, she would come out to the car and talk to Rose, helping her get out and into school. Sometimes it worked, and sometimes it did not. On days when Rose's anxiety was at its peak, I would take her to Target for a quiet walk around the store. Rose could talk through her feelings and not have to think about school. Being out of the house and away from the school environment gave her the space she needed to not feel anxious. It helped Rose manage her anxiety, and it also helped me. It reminded me that sometimes, taking a step away from the pressure of an every day routine could make all the difference for both of us.

Watching Rose go through all of this brought back memories of my own school days. I do not recall ever hearing the words "anxiety" or "anxious" growing up, but that's exactly what I had. I remember walking into middle school, and the sheer thought of seeing hundreds of kids, with their hundreds of eyes on me, would send me straight into panic mode. To cope, once my mom would drop me off, I would head straight to the bathroom, where I'd stay until the bell rang, just trying to catch my breath. This continued through junior high and high school. It was not until much later in life that I realized I had been dealing with anxiety, and back then, I did not know what to call it. I didn't give it another thought until I watched my own child living out my biggest fear. I had never fully acknowledged how deeply that anxiety had shaped my own experiences until I saw it mirrored in Rose. I never imagined my child, being diagnosed at just seven years old, would have to face the same struggles. But as I thought back to my own childhood, I now saw the earliest signs of my anxiety—at the same age Rose was diagnosed. It was eye-opening, but also deeply emotional, as I wished I had known sooner, both for my sake and for Rose's.

What's a Parent to Do?

At this time, Rachel was very aware of the extent of Rose's anxiety, and she was a true advocate. She knew how Rose felt because memories invaded her thoughts of her earlier days in school. Rachel knew that she had to be prepared for the ARD or IEP meeting, whatever the district called it. She went into the meeting with all of Rose's documentation; she knew the laws and rules, and she knew the rights that Rose had. She would not be intimidated at all.

She also provided all of us with a valuable lesson: When one writes to a particular staff member, such as the case manager, it is also advisable to copy other people. That way, the case manager could not ignore the letter, or if the case manager did so, someone else could respond. In this action, you also learned about the importance of holding all school personnel accountable for their actions.

In this section, an important lesson was learned: When your child becomes anxious, consider taking them to a neutral spot where you can talk with them without being threatened. Instead, listen to understand how your child feels.

Takeaways

1. Any correspondence that you send to school personnel should be copied to others in the school and you should always keep a copy. If someone on staff tells you they will do something, follow up with a written note that says: "As per our conversation, it is my understanding that my daughter will be able to see the social worker as needed." Again, keep a copy.
2. Take a copy of your child's records with you to the IEP meeting.
3. Recognize that some of the challenges your child is facing may trigger an unpleasant similar memory that you faced.

Chapter 11

Planning Ahead for Difficult Situations

Rachel's Story

Rose was starting her sophomore year in high school, and for the first time in many years, she would be without her sister Alexis, who had graduated. It was going to be a challenging year for her as she had to learn how to navigate high school without her biggest supporter. As her counselor had previously helped Rose with setting her schedule, he arranged for her to have lunch at the same time as her good friend. Going into a large cafeteria was hard for Rose due to her anxiety, but seeing a friendly face was comforting. Having that plan in place helped her feel better knowing she would have a friendly face to see in the crowd.

On the days when her friend was not at school, I would go pick Rose up without anyone seeing her, and we would head to the nearest fast food restaurant to grab a bite. We would park across the street at the bank and just sit, talk, and eat our lunch. A few minutes before the bell rang to signal the end of her lunch period, I would drive to the parking lot and park my car to avoid drawing attention to myself dropping her off. This became our new routine as I found myself picking her up a couple of times per week. Was I enabling her, maybe, but I know how badly she wanted to stay in school so she could graduate alongside her peers.

At the end of the last nine-week period of her sophomore year, due to the amount of days she had missed, Rose was in danger of failing some of her classes. After discussing the situation with her counselor and case manager, we decided that the best course of action would be to withdraw her from high school and have her finish the year at home through homeschooling. The decision was not easy, but we knew it was necessary to give Rose the best chance to succeed. I knew this is not something Rose would want, but we had to think of the bigger picture.

The biggest challenge my husband and I faced was explaining to Rose that we had to make this change in order to prevent her from failing her classes and being unable to start the next school year as a junior or participate in the swim team the following year. I knew this would be a tough conversation. Rose had worked so hard to be part of that school, and I did not want her to feel like she had failed in any way.

I met with Ms. Jones to discuss the new plan, and we decided to talk to Rose about it together. Ms. Jones had always been a supportive person to Rose, and I trusted her guidance during this transition. After talking about the pros and cons of the plan, Rose agreed that it was the best decision for her, though I could tell it was not easy for her to accept. We reassured her that this was not a setback, but rather a way to ensure she could get back on track and start the next year as a junior and to be able to stay on the swim team.

After gathering her belongings, we said goodbye to the school she had longed to be a part of. This was not what either of us had imagined, but we both knew it was the right choice. It was decided that the classes she was passing at the time of her withdrawal would count, but the ones she was failing (due to excessive absences) needed to be made up and passed in order for her to receive credit for her sophomore year. While I knew this change would be challenging for Rose,

I felt hopeful that, with the right support at home, she could finish strong and be ready for the next school year.

After researching the different curriculum options, I found a self-paced program for Rose to continue her studies. This program allowed Rose to work at her own pace, which took a lot of pressure off her. She could work through the material when she was ready as we did not have a set schedule. The flexibility gave her the control she needed to complete her studies. Rose chose to do her schoolwork in the evenings, allowing her to work when she felt more relaxed and focused. Over the course of the next few months, she was able to knock out the three classes she needed to finish by the end of the school year.

I was proud of how Rose handled being homeschooled again, even though it was not easy. There were times when she struggled with motivation, but having the flexibility to work at her own pace really made a difference. She passed her online courses and we were thrilled. Along with the classes she had taken at school, she would be ready to re-enroll by the fall. It was a huge sigh of relief to see her finish the year strong. My husband and I were confident that the experience had helped her grow, and that she would be ready for eleventh grade.

What's a Parent to Do?

During this year, Rachel did a wonderful job of foreseeing the problem that Rose might have now that her sister was no longer in the school so she worked out that Rose could have lunch with a friend. This alleviated some anxiety. This is so critical for parents to do—look ahead at what might be a problem and solve it in advance. Rose also eased back into classes. However, Rose became overwhelmed with the pressure of the classes. So the difficult decision was made that Rachel would homeschool Rose for the rest of the year so that she could receive her credits for the rest of the year. She passed her sophomore year.

Table 11.1
Supporting your child's emotional and academic success

Action	Why it matters
Anticipate potential challenges	Proactively identifying and addressing potential problems, such as social changes or anxiety triggers, helps prevent issues before they arise.
Facilitate social connections	Arranging for your child to spend time with a friend during potentially stressful situations, like lunch, can alleviate anxiety and provide emotional support.
Monitor academic pressure	Recognizing when your child is overwhelmed by academic demands allows you to make adjustments to protect their mental health and well-being.
Consider alternative education options	Flexible education solutions, such as homeschooling, can be a valuable option when traditional schooling becomes too stressful, ensuring your child can continue their education at a pace that works best for them.
Focus on long term goals	Use key milestones like passing the school year or mastering specific skills, as starting points to guide your child's progress. This approach helps break potentially overwhelming challenges into manageable steps while prioritizing your child's emotional well-being.

Takeaways

1. Sometimes parents have to make difficult decisions that the child needs a different kind of educational services. Parents should weigh all options and do what they believe is best for their child.
2. Plan ahead for problems that might appear that will cause your child's anxiety to increase.
3. Parents should always monitor undue pressures that the child may have.
4. Seek feedback from your child about what she sees as her needs so that the needs can be addressed with the school.

Chapter 12

Coping with Communication Breakdowns

Rachel's Story

Summer had come to an end, and it was time to gather all of Rose's paperwork to re-enroll her for her junior year. I had kept well-organized records of her schoolwork at home, so I did not anticipate any issues with her returning to school in a few weeks. I was hopeful that her transition back to school would go smoothly, and I had done everything I could to ensure she was ready. Her swim team had also resumed, and she was excited to reunite with her teammates. The sense of camaraderie and the routine of practice were things Rose looked forward to, and I knew being back on the team would be good for her both socially and emotionally.

I could not help but feel a mix of nervousness and optimism as we helped Rose prepare for the upcoming school year. I could only imagine what she was feeling as it had been almost six months since she left the school. I hoped this would be a fresh start for Rose, and I believed she was ready to go back to school and face whatever came her way. I was confident that with her strength, the support system we had in place, and determination, Rose was ready.

Rose's junior year started off much like her previous years, where her anxiety was extremely high. Once again, her counselor made sure she had the same lunch as her friend from last year. Creating a new routine was going to be a tough challenge, but we knew it was important for her to be successful in school. Her case manager and I had a plan to gradually reintroduce her to full-day classes. The plan worked for some time, but every school break seemed to bring setbacks. It was hard for Rose to stay in her classes for the entire day. I felt like no one truly understood the extent of my daughter's struggles and overwhelming feelings.

In April of her junior year, we scheduled Rose's ARD meeting that would carry her the rest of this year and into her senior year. We did not expect this one to be any different as this was possibly the last ARD she would have before graduating.

Rose had been struggling for so long to stay in school. She absolutely did not want to go back homeschooling. My husband and I discussed Rose having a modified day at school as an option and we thought it was a great plan. I had done my due diligence and researched how to put this plan in place. I scoured the Texas Education Agency's website and found the verbiage I needed to ask the ARD team to consider this as an option for Rose. So, I decided I would bring up this idea to the team and get their input. After all, if it was on the TEA website, then I'm sure this would be something they would support.

We have had the same people on Rose's ARD team that we have had since she started high school: Rose, myself, the special education coordinator, the school psychologist, one general education teacher, her case manager, and an assistant principal (although this was not an assistant principal we knew very well) assigned to her. Normally, her counselor would be in attendance, but I was told he would be late. Him not being there should have been a red flag for me, and I should not have let the meeting start without him.

At each IEP meeting, everyone had always been supportive of Rose, and had been in agreement with the modifications and accommodations she needed. Not much had changed in the last three years on her IEP. I'm not sure why this meeting would be any different, but it was a complete disaster that I did not see coming.

The meeting started off as usual with the reading of Rose's IEP that listed the supports she was receiving. As each person took their turn to talk about Rose, and how she was doing, it was not long before things started to go awry. This was an ARD meeting unlike any others. Everything started going off the rails as everyone (not her counselor as he was not there at the time) on Rose's team, started to walk back their support of her.

During the meeting, the vice principal (we had no prior contact with this person and did not know her before this meeting) mentioned that her attendance was "all over the place." Yes, some days, Rose would miss morning classes, and on other days, she would miss afternoon classes. Every day, she would get up, get dressed, and I would drive her to school, but sometimes, she would be unable to get out of the car due to her fear and anxiety. The vice principal's tone in which she was describing Rose's absences was as if she was trying to be funny. I don't know who she was pandering to but it was absolutely insulting. She brought up the idea that Rose could try to go to another school for anxious kids. Although, there was a catch, if she decided to go there, she would not be allowed back at this high school. I had already looked into this as an option, and it was a school for kids that had committed serious offenses, and would never be allowed back in a public school. This was the team's best idea, to send Rose to a place for delinquents? It was not a school for kids with anxiety, it was far from that. Of course, this was not something we would even consider. Rose wants to graduate from the same school that her brother and sister did, and I would do everything in my power to make that happen regardless of what the team wanted her to do.

I brought up the idea of having a modified school day with her only attending half days, and I was met with an emphatic, no. I should have told them that she does not choose when she has debilitating anxiety. She does not want a modified day because she is "bored" in her classes (as was referenced during the meeting). She wants a shortened day because she feels trapped. Telling her to go to class or sit in another room will not work as her anxiety would continue to manifest.

Rose's IEP was never discussed. They could only talk about how many days she had missed, and gave Rose the option to go to a different school. I don't know why we didn't discuss ideas on how to better support her. Why were they not offering accommodations or modifications that would help address her anxiety issues? The team began talking about Rose as if she was not sitting in the same room. I think I was in shock as it felt like a dream, or should I say nightmare that I could not wake up from. I trusted these people, and to watch them talk about my daughter like I was not there, was absolutely baffling.

I thought I knew everything I needed to know about ARD/IEP meetings, as I had been to quite a few over the years, but the weight that was put on me to sign the documentation stating that I agreed with what they were saying/suggesting, was overwhelming. I kept pushing back saying I did not think the decisions they were making for Rose were correct. I verbally reiterated that I did not want to sign the document. I felt as though the team was pushing for decisions that I knew were not in Rose's best interest, and there seemed to be little room for discussion about her unique needs. They reassured me that signing the documents was the right decision for Rose, but their words did not provide the comfort I needed. Absolutely nothing was accomplished at this meeting other than to tear Rose down, or so it seemed as it felt like she and I had been bullied. Not one thing was changed on her IEP, and I questioned why this was scheduled.

Even though I was hesitant, I signed the documents stating that I waived my 10-day waiting period. As I signed the paperwork, I said to them emphatically, out loud, that I did not agree with what they had decided. No one told me that I could have checked the box saying that I did not agree with the outcome of the meeting, a fact that I did not learn until later. Her counselor came into the room to share his thoughts on what would help Rose, but it was too late, the paperwork had been signed. He was the only one that was standing up for her, and I really appreciated that, but it would not have made a difference with this group.

I felt absolutely defeated, and I know Rose felt the same way. Her voice was not being heard, and neither was mine. I had been her biggest advocate for so long, and now my input was being dismissed. There was so much uncertainty about what the future held and I wondered if I had done the right thing for Rose.

As I sat looking around the table, no one noticed that Rose was gradually slumping into her chair. No one bothered to ask if she was alright or if she needed anything. She was experiencing an anxiety attack, and not one person said anything to her. Her case manager, the one person I thought would stand up for her, said, "See, this is what I deal with all the time," and it broke my heart. She was the person that had been with Rose since her freshman year, and she knew the struggles she faced day in and day out. I looked at Rose as her eyes were welling up with tears. I, too, felt the tears start to stream down my face. Everyone got up from their seats and left the room. No one seemed to have a heart that day, and I was appalled at their behavior. If I was being treated this way, what was it like for Rose? I looked at her and told her we were leaving. No one tried to stop me from taking her home. I learned all I needed to about the special education department that day. Rose and I both felt betrayed, but my heart hurt the most for her, as the one person she counted on had turned her back on her.

I had so hoped her case manager would reach out to Rose and let her know why she felt compelled to make fun of her during the meeting. Even a text that said she was sorry for her behavior, but she never spoke of what happened that day again. I wanted to call her and ask her why she acted the way she did, but Rose told me not to. Rose handled this situation with dignity and grace.

The next day, I received copies of the meeting notes and in the prior written notice, there were items left out and there was a false statement. I verbally, in front of the entire committee, excluding her counselor, Dr. Simon as he was not there at the time, disagreed with what the team had proposed for Rose, and that should have been written in the deliberations. As I was reading the paperwork, I learned the school psychologist called Rose's doctor to discuss her mental health condition and her medications without my consent. I was absolutely stunned by both parties that this took place without my knowledge. I had not signed anything from Rose's doctor allowing anyone from the school to access her medical records. Her doctor should have contacted me first, and I was absolutely fuming as I continued to read the report from the ARD meeting.

I told a friend, who was an educator about what happened during the ARD. She told me there should have been someone taking notes during our meeting. They would note my disagreement with what the committee wanted to put in place for Rose, but it was not in the documentation. Also, there was a statement that said Rose's doctor did not treat her for anxiety, which was not true. Rose's doctor did treat her for that condition and had given her medication for the diagnosis. Rose had only been part of Dr. Bell's practice for roughly one year, so the doctor does not necessarily have the prior knowledge of all that she has been through. I have years' worth of documentation of her mental health issues and learning disabilities.

After the ARD meeting, I felt extremely disheartened with the outcome, and how the committee acted towards Rose. I regretted not telling them how I failed my daughter by not acknowledging her strength, courage, and resilience in going to school with over 3000 kids. I should have told her how proud I was of her for facing her fears every single day. I realized that I should have fought harder, shared with everyone what a day in her life looks like, and made them see how much effort it took for her to just show up. I do not think it would have mattered to the committee. Ms. Jones, the one who knew Rose best, should have been the one to step up and show support for Rose, but she ended up mocking her instead.

I wish I had been more vocal about the struggles Rose silently carried. I felt guilty for not advocating more fiercely for her emotional and mental well-being, but it was a hard lesson. If they were able to understand her needs better and if I had spoken strongly about her challenges and her incredible perseverance, maybe there would have been a different outcome in the meeting. I replayed the meeting in my mind over and over, and I wished there had been a different outcome, but unfortunately, that was not the case.

I was not sure how we would move past this, but the one thing I did know is that Rose wanted to continue her studies and stay on the swim team at the school. There had to be some type of middle ground because I did not want to withdraw her again and start over as we have done so many times in the past.

I reached out to a friend and told her what happened in the meeting. She suggested I hire a special education advocate. I did not know anyone like this existed, but I decided to look more into it, and find her the best one I could.

I wasn't sure where to start, but I thought about looking on social media. After posting in one of the many support groups for parents of kids with anxiety, one name kept coming up: Mrs. Lincoln. Everyone seemed to have had positive experiences with her, and I felt a sense of hope as I read through the recommendations. I was thankful for all of the advice, and I felt a sense of relief knowing that other parents were going through the same thing. I realized how much I needed someone who understood advocacy and could advocate for my daughter. Although I had been through multiple ARDs, it would be helpful to have someone with superior knowledge. Mrs. Lincoln's stellar reputation reassured me that I was making the right choice. It was time to bring in someone who could advocate on behalf of Rose's needs.

I set up the meeting the following week with Mrs. Lincoln. As soon as we sat down, she assured me that I had her full support and that she would advocate on behalf of Rose. I was overwhelmed with emotion and it felt like we finally had someone who would guide us on what to do next. Mrs. Lincoln shared her knowledge of ARD meetings, and IEPs and it made me realize this is exactly what I had desperately been searching for. She listened intently to my concerns, and promised to ensure Rose's needs were met with the urgency and respect they deserved.

For the first time in a long time, I felt like someone truly understood the challenges Rose was facing, and Mrs. Lincoln was prepared to help her overcome them. It was a relief to have an advocate who had years of experience and could help us get Rose the help she needed in school. I left the meeting feeling that I was not in this alone. Rose's journey had been long and difficult, but with Mrs. Lincoln's support, I knew we were on the right path.

Mrs. Lincoln got to work immediately. She reviewed Rose's paperwork, contacted the school, and laid out exactly what needed to happen for Rose to get the support she deserved. The speed at which she got things done, blew my mind. This was a woman on a mission and I was glad she was on our team. I knew this was going to be a tough case for her, but Mrs. Lincoln was determined.

The care and detail with which Mrs. Lincoln handled this situation showed that she was not just doing this as a job; she truly cared about Rose's well-being. She kept me informed every step of the way making sure I was included in all of the decisions. For the first time in years, someone was actively working to ensure Rose had every opportunity to succeed. Mrs. Lincoln took the time to understand the challenges she was facing at school. Having her advocating for Rose's accommodations and modifications, would make a difference in her school life. My husband and I were relieved knowing that Rose's educational journey was being handled by someone with so much knowledge of the special education system.

Mrs. Lincoln was well known and had a stellar reputation and I like to think that is one of the reasons she was able to help us reconnect with the school and the ARD team. Everyone at the school that knew her, spoke very highly of her, so that was a definite bonus. Thanks to the efforts of Mrs. Lincoln and the ARD team, Rose was able to receive the necessary accommodations and modifications to successfully complete the school year. With their support,

Rose was able to earn the credits she needed to progress to twelfth grade. She was eagerly looking forward to attending upcoming senior events like the swim banquet, prom and graduation.

After experiencing an emotional rollercoaster with the latest ARD meeting and deciding to bring in an advocate, I contemplated how I could prevent other parents from facing the same situation, and that weighed heavily on me. I talked with my husband about how I could make a difference, I decided to enroll in a special education advocacy course to learn all I could about being an advocate. I believe there should be a stronger connection between the school and the parents, and that parents need to understand how an ARD meeting works. My goal is to empower parents, and the advocacy training would help me achieve that.

As I went through the training, I realized how much I had learned through my experiences with Rose. My goal was to help other parents who were struggling to understand their rights, and to help guide parents through the complexities of special education, from understanding IEPs and ARDs to knowing how to advocate for their child's needs. What we went through with Rose taught me that every parent deserves to be heard and supported in securing the right accommodations for their child.

What's a Parent to Do?

Rose's junior year started rocky with an ARD where staff lacked understanding of the turmoil that Rose faced. Every day was hard for her, and she struggled to make it through each day. The school staff seemed to have lost their empathy for her. At the ARD, Rachel advocated for her daughter and stood up for her rights. She was not told that she had the right to disagree with the decision of the group, so once she learned that she wrote a lengthy report stating what she believed would be most beneficial for Rose.

She also learned that the school had communicated with Rose's doctor without her permission. This was inappropriate, and as a result, there were major communication issues because the school did not understand Rose's needs. Did the school violate her right to confidentiality? Yes, they did and Rachel let them know that. Hopefully, the school learned a lesson from that and would not violate any other student's right to privacy. Rachel also lost trust in the school because they had not protected the rights of Rose.

At that point, Rachel hired an advocate to assist her through the process. There does come a time when a parent says, "I cannot do this alone. I need an outside advocate." Rachel had reached that point, and that helped her get through the days ahead. Trust had been broken and Rachel needed support.

Table 12.1
Navigating privacy concerns with schools

Action	Why it matters
Advocate for your child's rights	Standing up for your child during meetings, such as ARDs, ensures their needs are prioritized and their rights are upheld. Parents should also be aware of their right to disagree with decisions and provide written input when necessary.
Understand confidentiality laws	Knowing your child's privacy rights helps you identify and address violations, such as unauthorized communication with medical professionals, and ensures their confidentiality is protected.
Address broken trust	When trust is compromised, it's important to confront the issue directly and hold the school accountable to prevent future violations.
Seek professional advocacy support	Hiring an advocate can provide expertise and emotional support, especially when navigating complex situations or when trust with the school has been lost.
Recognize when you need help	Acknowledging that you cannot handle everything alone and seeking outside assistance ensures you have the resources and support needed to advocate effectively for your child.

Takeaways

1. The Individuals with Disabilities Education Act provides that supports for school personnel be written into the IEP. When parents suspect that personnel need training in working with students who have disabilities, they can specifically ask for training for staff.

2. It is critical that parents understand that school districts may not release information to outside agencies or persons without the written consent of the parent.

3. Seek the use of outside parent advocacy centers. IDEA provides for funded parent information and advocacy systems and those systems should engage in outreach to parents and parents utilize these free advocacy centers to help them in their journey to receive appropriate services for their child.

Chapter 13

The Importance of Endurance for Success

Rachel's Story

Rose had finally made it to her senior year with the goal of graduating from the same school as her siblings. She could see the top of the mountain she had been climbing for so long. However, as the year progressed, she faced several challenges. To ensure her graduation in May, her case manager, advocate, and I worked together to prioritize her attendance in all of her core classes. We knew she needed to attend all of her classes as it was critical to ensure that she would graduate. There were still days when Rose struggled with anxiety, making it difficult for her to get to school. With the support of her case manager and the accommodations in place, we were able to create a plan that worked.

Rose was looking forward to a new class she had thought about taking previously: theater arts. In the beginning of the year, she auditioned for show choir, and made it, but could not attend rehearsals because of her swim team practice schedule. I was surprised that she was interested in acting, as she never liked being in the spotlight. However, she decided to give it a try because she has always enjoyed writing and was fascinated by the process of making movies. If she did not like the class, she could always switch to another one since there were many options available to her.

Rose was thriving in her theater arts class. She had a group of friends who had formed a great connection. She had even written a play and was elected to be the director, and she was so excited for her debut that was coming up in a few weeks. Rose had finally found her group of peers and was having a wonderful senior year.

We had reached spring break of 2020, and we could see the light at the end of the tunnel to Rose's graduation day. She was set to make her directorial debut in her theater arts class after the break, and she would only have eight weeks of school left once she returned. Unfortunately, the rest of the school year turned out to be quite different from what we had imagined.

With news of what looked like a pandemic, there was so much uncertainty of what was to come next. All students were told to stay home until further notice. As the days turned into weeks, it became a waiting game to see if the schools would eventually reopen.

The pandemic would shut the world down. At first, we thought it would be a short break; two or three weeks at most, but as weeks turned into months, the reality set in. Rose and her classmates faced the disappointment of missing out on the milestones they had worked so hard to reach. Her directorial debut in theater arts was canceled, her swim season was cut short and her beautiful prom dress would hang in her closet, never to be worn.

There were many changes that had to be made especially for kids still in school. All classes were moved online, and there would be no going back to the campus. Despite all of this, Rose stayed resilient. She adapted to the new online learning environment, which she actually really enjoyed. Though all of the in-person events she had looked forward to were no longer happening, the school tried to find ways to celebrate the milestones of the seniors. It was not the graduation we imagined she would have, but Rose's journey had always been about perseverance and finding strength in the face of adversity. And, despite the challenges, she was ready to step into her future.

When the school administration realized that they were going to need to cancel the in-person graduation ceremony for the students, they devised a plan to ensure the kids could still have a meaningful graduation experience. We were told to expect an email for the date and time of Rose's individual graduation ceremony, and that only the people that lived in our house could attend the event. No other family would be able to attend. There would be no party to celebrate all of Rose's successes and hard work, and it was heartbreaking. But we did not let the situation get us down as we would plan a family celebration when we could all be together.

All of the individual graduations would take place at the high school. The principal, teachers and school staff tried to make it as fun as it could be even though it was not a traditional graduation. They made a small ceremony feel like a big production, and I know they had worked very hard to make this happen.

We watched as our girl received her well-earned diploma, and we took as many pictures as they would allow before they told us to move on. We were all just so excited for Rose! The ceremony from start to finish was about 15 minutes. Afterwards, we went to one of the only restaurants that was open and celebrated her huge accomplishment.

There are many teachers and staff deserving of our gratitude for their support of Rose throughout her school years. Their compassion and dedication played a vital role in her success and helping her achieve her goal of graduating.

As Rose's time in school has come to an end, I am in amazement at how far she has come. All of the adversity she faced, she did so with grace. From her initial diagnosis of anxiety and learning disabilities, and the struggles that followed, she never gave up. Rose found the strength to rise above her hardships. Her road was not an easy one, but she proved that anything is possible with perseverance, and dedication. Witnessing her face all the trials and tribulations showcased her inner strength. Rose's journey is just beginning, and I'm so proud to be her mother.

This book is intended to be a source of hope, guiding parents and caregivers to support their children. I know that I am my child's greatest advocate, and it's my aspiration that other parents realize they also have this strength within them.

What's a Parent To Do?

Rose did find success and looked forward to theatre arts. Then the pandemic struck, and things changed. Classes were online, but Rose very successfully completed her course requirements because the school cooperated with Rachel to see that Rose would meet her goal.

It was sad that the students had different graduation ceremonies; some got more recognition than others. But Rachel and her daughter focused on the big picture: Rose graduated from high school.

As you read this book, think about all of the many challenges that Rachel faced in ensuring that her daughter Rose's needs were met. There were lots of battles, but Rachel never gave up. She understood her daughter's challenges and accepted all of her daughter's strengths and interests. She capitalized on Rose's swimming and theater arts and was there every step of the way to ensure her daughter's success.

Rachel not only advocated for her daughter, but throughout Rose's school career, she also educated many of the staff members to give them a better understanding of how anxiety seriously impacts school performance. As a result of Rachel's advocacy and tireless efforts to educate the school staff, think of the positive ripple effect she had that made the lives of other children who continue to experience anxiety better. She made an impact on the lives of many other children. As parents struggle to get their children's services, they must be tireless and relentless. Rachel is a role model for all parents and educators.

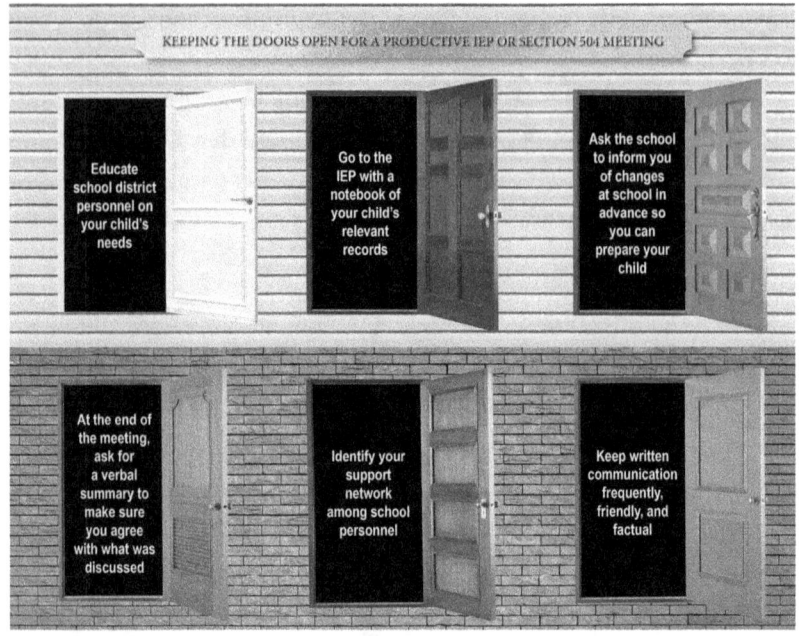

Figure 13.1
Keeping the doors open for a productive IEP or section 504 meeting.

Nick Manker at Production Xpress

Takeaways

1. Capitalize on your child's strengths throughout the process. Rose was interested in theater arts and there she found her niche for success.

2. Never give up on fighting for what your child needs. Keep the final goal in the front of your mind at all times.

3. Celebrate the many successes your child has along the way. Build them up and let them know that you are there for them all along the way.

Appendix

Checklist for Parents of Children with School Anxiety

Step 1: Meet with Your Child's School Team

- Email your child's teacher, the school counselor, and the special education team to set up a meeting.
- Once in the meeting talk about your child's strengths, challenges, and any specific needs they may have.

Step 2: Plan for Accommodations

Create a 504 Plan or IEP (if needed):
- If your child has not been evaluated, ask the school to perform an evaluation.
- Request the evaluation in writing to make it official.
- Work with the school to add accommodations like:
  - Ask for extra time on tests, and if need be, for the test to be read out loud.
  - Access to a quiet space or for your child to take sensory breaks.

- ◈ Visual schedules or calming tools.
- ◈ Ensure that all accommodations are well documented, and that everyone has a copy.

Step 3: Share Key Information

What to share:
- ◈ Information about things that might increase your child's anxiety.
- ◈ A list of strategies that help calm your child while at home.
- ◈ Any medical or psychological diagnoses that would help the team learn more about your child.

Step 4: Create a Routine for the Morning

Why it's important: A consistent morning routine can help reduce anxiety for your child to start their day.
- ◈ Tips for Success:
    - ◈ Have your child pick out their clothes the night before.
    - ◈ It is also a good idea to help them pack their lunch as the mornings can be hectic.
    - ◈ For younger children, it can be helpful to use a visual checklist for morning tasks
    - ◈ Plan to allow for extra time in the mornings to avoid rushing.

Daily Tips for Supporting Your Child with Anxiety in School

Why it's important: Daily conversations help you stay connected to your child.
- ◈ Ask open-ended questions like:

- "What was the best part of your day?"
- "What was the hardest part of your day?"
- Listen with empathy and let your child know it's okay to feel upset or frustrated.
- Your child might not want to talk for a bit after they get home from school and that's okay. They will come to you on their own time.

Build Relationships with School Staff

Why it's important: Regular communication is important to ensure that everyone is on the same page about your child's educational needs.

- Schedule regular check-ins with teachers, and their case manager (if they have one). You can send an email to check in and they can get back to you when it is a good time for them. Your child's teacher or case manager will not be able to always get back to you right away, so don't be upset or alarmed if you do not hear from them immediately.
  - Ask questions like:
    - "How is my child managing transitions during the day?"
    - "Are there specific situations that seem to trigger their anxiety?"
- If you know your child is having a bad day, it is a good idea to let their teacher know by sending an email in the morning before school.

Provide Updates to the School

Why it's important: Keeping the school informed regarding your child helps them provide better support.

- Decide what to share (share only what you are comfortable with).

- Provide updates about therapy or counseling sessions. You do not have to share any specifics of their counseling sessions, but letting the teacher or case manager know they are seeking outside treatment is beneficial.
- Let the school know about any changes in medication that might affect your child's focus, mood, or energy.
- Inform about significant events at home (e.g., moving, a family illness, or changes in routine).
- Please do not feel like you have to share anything regarding your child unless you think it will help the teacher or case manager understand your child.

Form a Partnership With your Child's School Team

Why it's important: Working together with the school team helps create a consistent support system for you and your child.

- When it comes to your child it is your right to ask questions about how your child will be supported in school.
- Ask for what strategies the school uses to manage your child's anxiety, and ask them to provide examples.
- Share what works well at home, like calming activities or specific rewards.

Encouraging Social and Academic Success

Foster Peer Connections

- Peer connections can be tough for a child that has anxiety. They may have a hard time making connections. Here are a few tips for fostering those relationships:
  - Building friendships can help your child feel more included and reduce anxiety.

- ❖ Encouraging your child to join a club, activity, or group that matches their interests will help them meet new people.
- ❖ Look for small-group activities where they can interact without feeling overwhelmed.
- ❖ Talk to the teacher or counselor about buddy systems or seating arrangements that encourage peer interactions.

Focus on Your Child's Strengths

- ❖ Celebrating your child's successes helps build their confidence and allows them to recognize their potential. Something that might seem small to you, could be something your child has worked on for a long time.
- ❖ It is important to praise their efforts, not just the results. Anxious children especially need to hear praise as they often have a lot of self doubt.

Help Your Child Stay Organized

Helping your child stay organized can reduce stress and can also help your child feel more in control while in school. Here are some tools to that could help with organization:

- ❖ Taking your child to the store to pick out a planner can be a great way to help them feel organized.
- ❖ Consider having them use colored folders or different colored notebooks for different subjects.
- ❖ For younger children, creating a visual schedule with pictures or symbols can help them feel less anxious and their tasks more manageable.
- ❖ Break larger tasks into smaller ones so your child will not feel overwhelmed.

Copyright material from Rachel Krueger and Beverley H. Johns, *Raising an Anxious Child*, 2026, Routledge

- Set up a dedicated workspace at home with the supplies they need to focus and do their schoolwork.

Coping Strategies for Anxiety at School

Teach Your Child Calming Techniques

Why it's important: Teaching your child to learn ways to self-soothe can help your child manage anxiety if they are feeling overwhelmed while at school.

- Tell them to take a moment and to count five things they can touch, see or hear.
- When feeling anxious, encourage them to visualize a safe, happy place like a favorite park or a place they like to visit.
- Let them know that asking for help when they feel overwhelmed is okay and is encouraged.

Create a Plan

Why it's important: Having a clear plan helps your child know what to do if they feel overwhelmed at school.

- Work with the School:
  - Meet with the teacher or counselor to develop a plan for moments of high anxiety. This might include:
    - Taking a short break in a quiet area.
    - Visiting the school counselor or nurse.
    - Using a special signal (like raising a colored card) to let the teacher know they need help.
    - If your child has a case manager, most of the time, they have their own room, and your child can go in there to decompress.

Copyright material from Rachel Krueger and Beverley H. Johns, *Raising an Anxious Child*, 2026, Routledge

- Discuss with Your Child:
  - Talk with your child about how to handle assignments that might overwhelm them.
  - Breaking larger assignments into smaller parts will help them feel less stressed.
  - Writing down questions to ask later if they do not understand something. If written into their IEP, class notes can be given to your child. Sometimes it is too much for them to be able to take notes and listen to the teacher at the same time.
  - Tell them to let the teacher know if they need more time or a different approach.
  - Reassure them that asking for help is okay and encouraged.
  - Explain to your child the plan with step-by-step instructions so they know what to do if they feel anxious.

Advocating for Your Child

Educate School Staff

Why it's important: Not all teachers or staff may fully understand how anxiety affects your child's learning and behavior. Sharing information helps them provide better support.

- Talk to the teacher about your child:
  - Explain how anxiety looks for your child. What happens when they get anxious.
  - Highlight what helps, such as calm reassurance or giving extra time.
  - Offer specific strategies that work well for your child.

Monitor and Make Adjustments

- ◈ Not all accommodations or strategies will be effective immediately. Adjustments will need to be made depending on the situation, and that can take time.
- ◈ Observations at Home:
  - ◈ Pay attention to how your child talks about school. Are they feeling less anxious or are they still facing difficulties?
  - ◈ Are they having a hard time going to school and staying for the full day?
- ◈ Request Changes:
  - ◈ If something is not working, ask for changes to be made that will benefit your child during their school day. You can ask for another IEP meeting and request new accommodations and/or modifications be put in place.
  - ◈ Be specific about what's not working and suggest alternatives that would benefit your child during their school day.
  - ◈ Keep all documents pertaining to parent/teacher meetings or IEP/504 meetings.

Self-Care for Parents

Practice Self-Care

- ◈ It can be emotionally draining to take care of a child with anxiety. It is easy to become overwhelmed, so remember to take care of yourself, too.
- ◈ Look for online or local groups focusing on special education or childhood anxiety.
- ◈ Make Time for Yourself:
  - ◈ Call a friend and ask if they would like to go on a short walk.

- ◆ Read a book, exercise, or partake in one of your favorite hobbies.
- ◆ Sometimes you can feel guilty about taking time for yourself. Do not feel guilty about having alone time to do something for yourself.

Stay Informed

- ◆ Learning more about anxiety will help you to advocate for your child and find effective strategies.
- ◆ Look for resources on childhood anxiety or special education.
- ◆ Stay updated by following groups on social media about kids that have anxiety, child psychologists, or advocacy organizations on social media.

Checklist for Parents of Children with Anxiety to Share with the School

- ◆ If possible, schedule a meeting with your child's teacher to discuss your child's needs, triggers, and what strategies are successful.
- ◆ Share any documents such as a 504 Plan, IEP, or doctor's notes (if you want to share), outlining your child's needs and accommodations.
- ◆ Visiting the campus where your child will be attending school before the start of the year will help them feel more at ease on their first day of school.
- ◆ Maintain regular communication with your child's teacher, Case Manager, Special Education Coordinator (if they have an IEP or 504), and their school counselor.

Copyright material from Rachel Krueger and Beverley H. Johns, *Raising an Anxious Child*, 2026, Routledge

- Let the school know if there are updates to your child's health or family situation that may affect their anxiety. Remember, you share only what you want to that you feel would benefit your child.
- It is important to establish routines for sleep, homework, and morning preparation. Routines work best for children with anxiety and learning disabilities.
- Discussing any changes with your child ahead of time, such as a new schedule or something that could potentially disrupt their day will help them feel better prepared.
- It is important to talk with your child's teachers and if they have one, a case manager to address anxiety-related absences and encourage consistent attendance.
- Using Organizational Tools can effectively help your child stay organized. Help your child pick out a planner to create checklists, or use digital tools to stay organized.
- Encourage your child to participate in activities or clubs to build friendships in a low-pressure environment. Ask your child what their interests are and see if the school offers a program they could join.
- If they are old enough, teach your child how to communicate their needs and advocate on their behalf to their teachers.
- Encourage your child to practice breathing exercises, mindfulness, or other strategies they can use at school to manage anxiety.
- Role play scenarios where your child might feel anxious and needs to leave the classroom.
- Create a calm, and quiet area at home where your child can decompress after school. Whether that be in their room or a place in your house where they feel comfortable.

- Form a partnership and collaborate with your child's teachers, Case Manager, and their school counselor to implement and adjust accommodations as needed.
- Reinforce the same strategies and expectations at home that are used at school to provide consistency.
- Communicate what works best for your child with the school so they can apply these strategies to support them while at school.
- Use available resources like counseling services, social skills groups, or tutoring to help your child while at school.
- If needed, ask the school about referrals to external therapists or mental health resources. You can also contact your child's doctor for more
- Celebrate your child's efforts and progress, regardless of how small they seem.

Checklist for School Personnel When Working Together with Parents of a Child with Anxiety

- Offer to meet with the parent(s) and school staff who work with the child before the school year starts. If the 504 plan or the IEP needs to be reviewed and revised, do so before school starts.
- Listen to understand what the parent is saying, not to respond.
- Provide positive comments to parents. They may be very stressed and need people who will recognize what they are doing right. Praise them for positive suggestions and their

willingness to work with you. Never dismiss their ideas. Talk more about why they may or may not work.

- Ask the parent for suggestions on what works for them.
- Make sure the parents feel comfortable at any school meeting.
- Avoid arguing with the parent. Work to recognize their point of view.
- If discussions begin to get tense during a meeting with the parent, have a short recess to try to diffuse any problems.
- Let the parents know that it is okay to bring a friend or advocate with them.
- Be open to allowing a parent to record the meeting if permitted by state law and school policy. The other parent may not be able to attend but would still like access to what was discussed. Sometimes, the attending parent may feel anxious, worried they might miss something the non-attending spouse would want to know.
- If possible, in a 504 meeting or an IEP meeting where someone is typing on their laptop, connect that laptop to a projector so everyone can see what is being written and whether the information is accurate.
- Stress that you want to work together to help the child.
- When the child has a good day at school or does something noteworthy, like passing a difficult test, or is having a good day, call or email the parent or send a positive note to celebrate the success. The parent needs to hear that their child is successful.
- Establish a designated contact person for parents to contact when issues arise. This could be the child's teacher (or a certain teacher if they have more than one), or case manager, if they have one. They should focus on building a positive relationship with the parent. When the child begins to have

problems, schedule either a parent conference, a 504 meeting, or an IEP. Avoid waiting until a problem escalates. Work to resolve issues before they become significant problems that affect the child.

- ❖ When the parent expresses frustration, ask how you can help. Sometimes, the parent just needs to know that you will support them.
- ❖ Educate all staff who work with the child on the need for accommodations and/or modifications.

Bibliography

Individuals with Disabilities Education Act (IDEA). "Sec. 300.320: Definition of Individualized Education Program." https://sites.ed.gov/idea/regs/b/d/300.320.

Lavoie, Richard. "How Difficult Can This Be? The F.A.T. City Workshop." www.ricklavoie.com/videos.html.

Navigate Life Texas. "Admission, Review, and Dismissal (ARD) Process." www.navigatelifetexas.org/en/education-schools/ard-process.

Partners Resource Network. "Other Health Impairment (OHI)." https://prntexas.org/other-health-impairment-ohi.

Partners Resource Network. "What Is a REED?" https://prntexas.org/what-is-a-reed.

Understood. "What is a 504 Plan." www.understood.org/en/articles/what-is-a-504-plan.

U.S. Department of Education. "Disability Discrimination: Providing a Free Appropriate Public Education (FAPE)." www.ed.gov/laws-and-policy/civil-rights-laws/disability-discrimination/disability-discrimination-key-issues/disability-discrimination-providing-free-appropriate-public-education-fape.

U.S. Department of Education. "Individuals with Disabilities Education Act." https://sites.ed.gov/idea.

U.S. Department of Education. "Protecting Students with Disabilities." www2.ed.gov/about/offices/list/ocr/504faq.html.

U.S. Department of Education. "Section 1412 (a) (5): Least Restrictive Environment." https://sites.ed.gov/idea/statute-chapter-33/subchapter-ii/1412/a/5.

For Product Safety Concerns and Information please contact our EU representative GPSR@taylorandfrancis.com
Taylor & Francis Verlag GmbH, Kaufingerstraße 24, 80331 München, Germany

www.ingramcontent.com/pod-product-compliance
Lightning Source LLC
Chambersburg PA
CBHW061420300426
44114CB00015B/2007